MANAGED TRADE

MANAGED TRADE
The New Competition Between Nations

RAYMOND J. WALDMANN

BALLINGER PUBLISHING COMPANY
Cambridge, Massachusetts
A Subsidiary of Harper & Row, Publishers, Inc.

International Standard Book Number: 0-88730-143-6

Library of Congress Catalog Card Number: 86-17231

Printed in the United States of America

Library of Congress Cataloging in Publication Data

Waldmann, Raymond J.
  Managed trade.

  Bibliography: p.
  Includes index.
  1. Commercial policy. 2. Free trade and protection—
Protection. 3. Competition, International. I. Title.
HF1411.W295   1986   382'.3   86-17231

  ISBN 0-88730-143-6

CONTENTS

PREFACE

The basic principle of free trade, the premise upon which all others rest, is that traders, businessmen, and investors should be able to make decisions based on market signals, with little or no interference from governments. The United States has continued to support free trade as the surest route to economic efficiency and increased general welfare. We continue to act as if all other countries adhered to our belief in the rightness of free trade.

But the postwar period has seen another development as important as the expansion of trade. That development is the growth of managed trade — the conscious control of trade and investment by governments. All governments, even those with highly capitalistic domestic markets, intervene in international economic matters in a wide and bewildering variety of ways. A large and increasing proportion of trade and investment is managed by governments.

Japan is noted for its ability to control both imports and exports; its spectacular growth encourages imitation. Many others attempt to manage trade, but few succeed as well. All East bloc communist countries control trade, for example, but their economies suffer for it. The prominence of barter, countertrade, and other government trade-balancing policies demonstrates yet another way governments intervene.

Trade in important sectors and commodities has increasingly become managed. OPEC manages, or attempts to manage, trade in the most essential of raw materials, crude oil. Trade in other basic commodities such as copper, sugar, coffee, tea, cocoa, and tin is ruled by government agreements that set price and quantity. Agreements control trade in textiles and apparel, automobiles, steel, electronics, aircraft, and a host of other products and services.

I have seen these developments firsthand during the last two decades. During the last half of the 1960s, I was a consultant working both with American firms establishing their first overseas operations and with the foreign governments that sought to attract them. These were the high-water years of American managerial optimism, the years when American technology and expertise were being applied and emulated everywhere.

During my first government job in 1970, as a staff assistant to the president, I worked on a variety of issues that brought home to me the enormous involvement of governments in international economic matters. It ranges from the global issues of foreign affairs to the nitty-gritty of trade promotion, agricultural surplus sales, trade disputes, and export finance for individual projects. During this time I worked with Pete Peterson, then Director of the Council on International Economic Policy (and later Secretary of Commerce) to draft the first government report on the subject of our international economy in 1971, still regarded as a pioneering effort. When I moved to the State Department, I was thrown into three of the most contentious areas of government involvement — aviation, shipping, and communications — where foreign governments have substantial ownership. Most recently, as Assistant Secretary for International Economic Policy, I participated in most of the major trade decisions of President Reagan's first term.

The basic conclusion I have reached from this experience is that all governments, the United States included, challenge the free trade system. We act, for the best of motives, to make the attainment of free trade impossible. Free trade depends on a series of prerequisites — that borders be open, that tariffs and other barriers to trade be reduced or eliminated, that investment flow without hindrance, and that economic efficiency rather than political expediency guide trade and investment decisions. Today none of these conditions has been fulfilled. As a result, we face unprecedented problems of trade policy that will call for dramatic solutions.

In the face of these developments the United States has held fast to the notion that managed trade is the exception rather than the rule.

We continue to urge free trade as the best policy for all countries because it has worked for us. In a sense, our adherence has provided a "nuclear" free trade umbrella allowing other countries to have it both ways — free access to the United States, the largest market in the world, while developing their own markets according to managed trade principles.

We must carefully examine the strategies and tactics of our trading partners and competitors. We must look at the "rules of the game" to test their fairness and biases, making sure our own house is in order and our own laws up to the challenges ahead. We must consider the role of international trade, finance, and development organizations in directing and influencing trade. And we must recognize, most importantly, the implications of the growing government involvement in international trade for our relations with other countries, especially those in North America, and those which also advocate free trade.

Should we continue to espouse a policy of free trade with fewer and fewer adherents? Or should we retreat behind protectionist walls? Are these the only two choices open to us?

I believe there is a middle ground for the United States of a realistic managed trade policy based on reciprocity. We can wisely and consciously use access to our market power to achieve wider adherence to free trade. Moreover, we should take the initiative to form a U.S.-led free trade bloc. The trade arrangements flowing from these policies would be consistent with our international obligations and the realities of today's world. These arrangements would build on the successes of the postwar trade agreements and would form the trade agenda for the United States for the remainder of this century.

ACKNOWLEDGMENTS

As in any work of this type, the debts owed to teachers, advisors, associates, and mentors extend over decades and would make dull reading for all except those mentioned. And what about those left out? My solution is simple—I gratefully acknowledge first, the support and advice of my wife Mary who suffered through my late nights and weekends at the computer; and second, the help of my colleagues in government and in Washington, D.C., who reviewed the manuscript and offered criticism: Harvey Bale, Michael Czinkota, Bo Denysyk, Gary Horlick, Tim Houser, Peter Levine, Tom McVey, and Clyde Prestowitz. To all others who have influenced this work in one way or another, you have my gratitude for your time and energies educating and guiding me this far, but I hereby release you from any responsibility for the product, which must of necessity remain with me.

INTRODUCTION

1 WORLD TRADE TODAY

International trade and investment have increased dramatically in the last forty years. The growth of world trade has surprised even the experts as new products are exported, new countries develop new industries, and new patterns of trade emerge. In the last two decades alone, from 1960–1980, world trade has expanded from $200 billion to over $2000 billion, a tenfold increase. The United States, along with all other traders, benefited from this growth.

Not only has trade mushroomed but its importance has increased. In 1960 exports as a percentage of the world's gross national products amounted to about 8 percent. Today the percentage is more than 16 percent, having doubled in just twenty years. Most countries are increasingly attentive to international competition, trade relations, and the rules governing trade and investment.

In no other country is this increased awareness more evident than in the United States. Today its international standing is discussed on the editorial pages, debated in Congress, and demagogued on the campaign trail. Of growing concern are the perils of the trade deficit, the consequences of jobs lost to foreign competition, the impact of possible default by foreign borrowers, and the need for an effective U.S. response.

Yet much of this debate is uninformed about the true nature of the challenge facing the United States. Fundamental trends affecting the future have yet to be grasped. The United States has been lulled into a false sense of security by the very enormity of its domestic economy and the outstanding results of the postwar period. These safety nets, however, may not alone be enough to sustain the country in the years ahead.

The trade policy problem facing the United States can be simply stated: Whether to adhere to the policies of the past in the expectation that they will continue to be effective, or to consciously adopt new strategies to deal with the changing world. This is the fundamental dilemma of today's policymakers. It arises in many forms and contexts and affects a vast number of decisions, policies, and practices. The analysis that follows draws basic conclusions about U.S. trade policy for the remainder of this century.

FUNDAMENTAL TRENDS IN THE INTERNATIONAL ECONOMY

The trade policy problem is better understood by first noting some of the factors influencing the international economy. One of the most significant trends has been the almost universal spread of manufacturing technology, skills, and management — referring not to the most advanced scientific developments, but rather to the stuff of day-to-day production. For example in 1965 the proportion of scientists and engineers in the U.S. workforce was three times that of Japan; today the proportion is roughly equal (Samuelson 1984). Europe and Japan now account for a majority of U.S. patents issued. In developing countries engineers and technicians are graduating in numbers that far exceed available jobs. Techniques, skills, machines, processes, even "trade secrets" appear wherever entrepreneurs have the vision and the initiative to use them.

As this technology spreads, local businessmen and investors realize the benefits of moving into higher value-added products that command higher prices in the markets of the world. No longer are nations satisfied to be the exporters of commodities, low-wage, or low value-added products alone. They also seek to upgrade their economies, improve their industries, and earn more foreign exchange through higher value-added production. This has enormous ramifications for education and training, development strategies, scientific exploration, and of course trade. All of these goals are a part of the overarching goal of many countries to industrialize as rapidly as possible.

The third fundamental trend occurring as a result of the spread of technology and the pressures to industrialize is the increasing freedom felt by nations to choose their economic futures. Much of this freedom is misperceived; countries cannot have a completely free choice and must be limited by their resources, their people, and their history. Nevertheless, more and more countries are misled by the promises of planners, the notion of directed economies, and the false premise of creating an economic comparative advantage that will lead to success in the international marketplace.

Consider for example the notion that government support for a research center on computers will allow any country to compete successfully in this fast-changing industry. By creating "comparative advantage" in this sector, the research center is expected to flourish and even export. Other, less favored sectors may fail, but that is accepted as the cost of staying abreast of the latest technology. Yet experience in many industries, including the computer industry itself, shows the folly of relying on such financial patronage unless the fundamental factors also support the health of the industry. This is an extensive problem only touched on here, but one of the most important aspects of government thinking about its role in industrial planning, and thus in international trade.

The fourth trend is the increasing tendency of governments to intervene in international trade. In its most extreme form, government management challenges the basic assumption of free trade on which postwar trade has been built. This assumption, embodied in treaties and international organizations, is that the private sector maximizes the public welfare by acting in its own self-interest and without government direction or control.

The U.S. faces these fundamental challenges to its economic position, yet simple solutions abound. For example, conventional wisdom states that the dollar's high purchasing power causes most of the symptoms of economic concern, and its fall will eliminate them. The determination of the true impact of the dollar on the international trade position of the United States is beyond the scope of this book. The analysis herein does not rely on the short-term and transient phenomenon of the high value of the dollar relative to historic values as the major cause of problems, nor will these problems be cured by a "return" to more "normal" values.[1]

THE UNITED STATES AS TRADER

The trend toward government management of trade and investment will influence every person in the United States. The United States now relies on international trade for about 14 percent of its GNP. Consider just a few indications of our reliance on trade:

- 1 of every 4 U.S. farm acres produces for export
- 1 of every 9 U.S. manufacturing jobs produces for export
- 1 of every $7 of U.S. sales is to a foreigner
- 1 of every 5 cars, 9 of every 10 television sets, half of all shoes, 2 of every 3 suits, and every video recorder sold in the United States is imported
- 1 of every $4 of U.S. government bonds and notes is issued to foreigners to finance the deficit

Without foreign earnings on overseas investments, the U.S. payments deficit would be three times as large. This reliance on international trade and investment must be considered by every citizen before voting, by every politician before legislating, by every businessperson before planning or investing for the future.

The United States is by far the largest trading nation in the world. In 1982 the United States exported $230.0 billion and imported $254.9 billion worth of merchandise.[2] U.S. exports that year amounted to 13.5 percent of the world's exports, which was 20.3 percent or one-fifth of the exports of the twenty industrial countries. The next largest exporters that year were West Germany ($138.2 billion), Japan ($114.0 billion), France ($113.9 billion), the United Kingdom ($93.9 billion), Italy ($76.2 billion), the Netherlands ($73.6 billion), Belgium ($56.9 billion), Canada ($48.4 billion), Saudi Arabia ($37.6 billion) and the USSR ($35.9 billion).

Exports from all thirty-three countries of Asia, excluding Japan, amounted to $150.0 billion. All of South and Central America exported $90.7 billion, and Africa $45.9 billion (not including the oil-exporting countries in those regions). The oil-exporting countries together accounted for $144.2 billion of the world's trade. U.S. exports were only slightly less than those of the next two largest exporters (Germany and Japan) combined, twice those of Japan, only slightly less than those of Asia and the Americas combined, and over six times more than those of the world's second largest economy, the USSR.

The aggregated exports of the ten countries of the European Economic Community amount to slightly more than 50 percent more than those of the United States.[3]

Although the United States has the largest export volume in the world, that volume is nonetheless a smaller proportion of total production than for most trading countries. As a percent of GNP, U.S. exports amount to only 5.9 percent compared with 12.4 percent in Japan, 17.9 percent in France, 19.8 percent in the United Kingdom, and 25.7 percent in Germany. For many other countries, both developed and underdeveloped, the proportion is even higher, especially in one-export countries. This explains why until recently, Americans considered international trade a comparatively obscure subject.[4]

The United States is also the largest importer, accounting for about 13 percent of the world's imports. For a large number of countries, the U.S. world share is even greater: In 1982, for example, the United States bought 16 percent of India's exports, 18 percent of Indonesia's, 20 percent of Brazil's, 26 percent of Japan's, 32 percent of the Philippines', 44 percent of Nigeria's, 56 percent of Mexico's, 65 percent of Canada's, and 78 percent of Haiti's. The United States buys twice the share of imports from developing countries that Europe does and 7.5 times as much as Japan does (*U.S. News World & World Report* 1985). Among the industrial countries, the United States imports the highest proportion of developing countries' products. These include many of the raw materials, commodities, textiles, footwear, and other manufactured products upon which their survival depends. Through these purchases the United States supports firms, industries, and even entire economies throughout the world. This is the most effective form of aid and assistance possible.

For decades the purchases of the United States have been the "economic locomotive" pulling many countries out of recessions and spurring growth in sluggish economies. The return from the 1981–83 recession is no different. The United States has run an unprecedented trade deficit with the rest of the world. With imports over $100 billion more than exports in 1984, business opportunities and jobs were ensured for all those supplying the U.S. market.

In 1985 the United States ran merchandise trade deficits with most of its trading partners (see Tables 1 and 2). Furthermore, the trade balances were worsening with every region of the world except the communist countries (*Business America* 1985). U.S. trade deficits mean prosperity for foreign exporters. In fact, this trade impact far exceeds

Table 1–1.   U.S. Balance of Trade (billions of dollars).

	Merchandise Trade Balance [a]	Manufactured Goods Trade Balance	Balance on Current Account [b]
1978	− 39	− 12	− 15
1979	− 42	− 2	− 1
1980	− 40	13	2
1981	− 36	5	6
1982	− 43	− 11	− 8
1983	− 69	− 38	− 46
1984	− 123	− 89	− 107
1985	− 149	− 113	− 110 [c]

a. Includes all trade in goods (agriculture, minerals, manufacturing products).

b. Includes merchandise trade, services trade, investment income, unilateral transfers, military transfers.

c. Based on first three quarters.

Source: Attachment to a letter dated February 5, 1986, from Chairman Dan Rostenkowski to members of the U.S. House of Representatives Committee on Ways and Means.

government assistance and military spending abroad, private investment flows, and voluntary contributions.

COMPETITION FROM ABROAD

The impact of international trade is not, of course, evenly dispersed throughout the economy. For U.S. industry as a whole, approximately 14 percent of output is exported. Some industries are much more dependent on foreign markets. For example, about 18 percent of farm machinery and 26 percent of computers are exported, above the average for all U.S. industry. Even higher shares are reached in turbines (32 percent), construction machinery (43 percent), and oilfield machinery (63 percent). In agriculture, 40 percent of wheat and 60 percent of soybeans and their products are exported.

As Gilder points out, the United States applied high technology 50 percent faster than either Europe or Japan. It has been able to export to the bastion of high technology protectionism, Japan, in spite of a high dollar: gains in sales over the last four years were 48 percent in computers, 38 percent in telecommunications equipment, 51 per-

Table 1–2.   Bilateral U.S. Merchandise Trade Balance (billions of dollars).

	1983	1984	1985
Canada	− 14	− 21	− 22
Western Europe	− 1	− 13	− 28
Japan	− 22	− 37	− 50
Mexico	− 8	− 6	− 6
Taiwan	− 7	− 11	− 13
Republic of Korea	− 2	− 4	− 5

Source: Attachment to a letter dated February 5, 1986, from Chairman Dan Rostenkowski to members of the U.S. House of Representatives Committee on Ways and Means.

cent in analytical instruments, 41 percent in pharmaceuticals, and 63 percent in electronic parts (Gilder 1985).

On the other hand, there are tremendous gains made by imports to the U.S. economy. Some industries suffer from foreign competition to a much greater degree than others. Over twenty percent of all automobiles sold in the United States are imported, a higher percentage than in any other automobile-producing country. Greater import shares are found in cameras, footwear, household electronics, watches, hand-held computers, and many other fields. Large industries like steel, autos, copper mining, and textiles and even small and varied industries like clothespins, mushrooms, metal fasteners, and specialty catalytic metals have felt the weight of imports. These industries have complained to the government for protection from imports and for assistance. Their pleas have driven the United States to intervene in trade as never before.

Even the biggest and best companies are large-volume importers of components and supplies. The IBM Personal Computer, a vivid example of successful product innovation and marketing, contains about 60 percent foreign material. Had IBM and others in the computer industry not imported, particularly from Japan, the rapid strides evident in that industry would not have been made. Despite its importance in world trade, the United States has not achieved a trade surplus since 1971. To many this suggests that the basic competitiveness in many export industries is eroding from this influx of imports. In fact the deficit in merchandise trade has grown alarmingly from

$32 billion in 1982 to $58 billion in 1983 to $100 billion in 1984. Part, but only part, of this merchandise deficit is now being offset by net earnings on services and income from investment abroad. This leaves the United States with worrisome payments deficit overall, an inherently unstable situation.

Compounding the problem is the uneven trade pattern. In 1982 the United States had a slight surplus with Europe (plus $2 billion), substantial deficits with Japan (minus $20 billion) and Canada (minus $14 billion), a small surplus with the communist countries (plus $2 billion), and deficits with the OPEC countries (minus $8 billion) and the other developing countries (minus $22 billion). A few years ago it enjoyed surpluses in capital goods and food and beverages, but deficits in consumer goods, automotive vehicles, and petroleum and petroleum products. In the miscellaneous industrial supplies category, the United States just about broke even. While trade was expanding and trade deficits were reaching record levels, the United States was able nevertheless to generate over 21 million new jobs during the ten years, 1975 to 1985 — maintaining the most open economy in the world (Baldrige 1985).

One popular myth is that the United States is helpless in the face of an onslaught of unfairly traded imports. Although the trade laws could be substantially improved, significant legislation already is in place:

- Antidumping statutes prevent imports from being priced below fair market value.
- Countervailing duty statutes add U.S. duties to imports that are sold with the aid of foreign export subsidies.
- Trademarks, copyrights, and patents are protected from foreign infringement or violation.
- Section 301 of the Trade Act of 1974, recently strengthened, allows a variety of actions (such as excluding their products) against countries pursuing "unfair trading practices."
- The Ex-Im Bank can finance U.S. exports that are competing with subsidized foreign products going to other countries.
- Domestic regulations for such industries as banking, shipping, aviation, and telecommunications can be used to respond to dumping or other unfair practices.

While U.S. trade was expanding, so was U.S. investment abroad. The period from 1950 through the 1970s was a boom era for U.S. com-

panies setting up shop overseas.[5] Investment is of two types, portfolio and direct. *Portfolio investments* are stocks, bonds, commercial paper, government securities, and similar readily salable or trans-
ferable paper. In contrast, *direct investments* are "real" investments
that include the control of companies, new plants and factories, and
real estate developments. Direct foreign investment was heavily concentrated in oil chemicals, machinery manufacturing, and a few other
industries and in a relatively select group of countries; but no country or industry was excluded from some U.S. investment. The dividends and other payments received from these investments have been
a large part of the nation's positive cash flow. Roughly 35 to 40 percent of U.S. imports and exports moved within multinational companies (MNCs) ("The World's In-House Traders" 1986: 61).

The United States clearly benefited from MNC operations through
the repatriation of earnings, the increased profits of U.S. investors,
and even increased exports. The Commerce Department reports that
in 1981, for example, $80.3 billion of U.S. exports went to U.S. com-
panies abroad. If those subsidiaries and operations were owned by
nationals of other countries, their purchases from the United States
would undoubtedly have been much lower ("The World's In-House
Traders" 1986: 61).

The host countries in which U.S. investment occurs have also benefited in many ways, so the bargain has not been one sided. Investment
means new jobs, transfer of technology, development of unused resources, expansion of their support economies, and training of local
managers and workers. Increasingly, critics of U.S. multinational companies in developing countries are realizing this. They consciously are
toning down their antibusiness rhetoric as they too seek to attract new
foreign investors.

Foreign investment in the United States remained at relatively low
levels until the 1970s, when it too exploded. The United States took
part in a worldwide investment expansion, chiefly conducted by the
largest multinational firms, which account for the bulk of the investment. The largest 500 multinational firms (many but not all of which
are U.S.-based) control about 80 percent of the approximately 90,000
affiliates established throughout the world (Rutter 1984). The United
States is the largest single country contributing foreign investment,
but its share of the world's total has declined from about 50 percent
in 1960 to close to 40 percent by 1981. The rate of foreign direct investment in the United States peaked in 1981 and declined in 1982

and 1983, but regained in 1984. In every year since 1980, the amount of foreign investment in the United States exceeded U.S. investment abroad.

One of the frequently cited indicators of the decline in U.S. competitiveness is its turnaround from a net lender to a net borrower during 1985. For the first time since 1919 the United States has become a debtor country. In 1984 the United States borrowed nearly $94 billion from foreigners, the largest such influx since immediately after the Civil War. Economists were predicting that by the end of 1985 the United States would be the largest foreign debtor at $100 billion, exceeding the $90 billion currently owed by Brazil (New York Times 1985).

The new development has been the substantial decline in U.S. funds going abroad. In 1983 the net investment position of the United States abroad dropped $44 billion, the first drop since 1977. In the past, earnings from foreign investments offset trade deficits. But now those earnings are not enough to cover the deficits, and without new investment overseas, they will not generate the income needed to offset future deficits in merchandise trade. This is a primary concern of U.S. economists today.

But the average citizen has not been concerned, having enjoyed the benefits of imported consumer products and the improved U.S. economy resulting from both portfolio and direct foreign investment. Foreign investment has found its way into almost every corner of American life. Direct investments in the United States increased by 92 percent between 1980 and 1984 (Volpe 1986). Not only are obviously foreign firms like Volkswagen and Nissan setting up operations in the United States but many U.S. companies now have substantial foreign owners or partners. American Motors is owned by Renault of France; A&P Foods is a subsidiary of Tengelmann of Germany; the Pan-Am Building in New York is owned by British interests; Santa Fe Drilling, a major oil industry service company, is owned by the Kuwait Oil Company; the major retailers Gimbels and Marshall Fields are owned by B.A.T. Industries of London; and large proportions of Miami condominiums, downtown Washington, D.C., Iowa farmland, and Honolulu business are now in foreign hands. By 1983, 7 percent of all U.S. manufacturing workers were employed by foreign-owned or foreign-affiliated firms (Volpe 1986).

Given the pressures abroad that have led to this investment, there is not likely to be a significant slowdown in foreign investment. Many

Europeans are concerned about the slow growth of their own economies, creeping socialism in their politics, and even the possibility of
direct Soviet action in Western Europe. The OPEC countries have
had to find safe and reliable havens for their enormous disposable
wealth. Asian and Latin American businesses have sought to invest
their savings in politically stable, economically sound, and commer-
cially profitable investments available in the United States as nowhere
else.

THE CHALLENGE AHEAD

Of course the growth of U.S. trade and investment has not occurred in
a vacuum. Many countries have not only shared in this growth but surpassed it. The GNP of the United States grew 2.5 percent annually during the 1970s and early 1980s, and those of Germany, France, and Canada had similar growth rates. Japan's rose at an annual average rate
of over 3.5 percent, and those of the rapidly industrializing world –
Korea, Brazil, Taiwan, Singapore, and Hong Kong – grew at even
faster rates, from 8 to 10 percent annually ("Global Competition"
1985). The major industrial and newly industrializing countries have
led the way, but much of the rest of the world has followed.

   As a result of the relatively faster rates of growth elsewhere, the
U.S. share of the world economy actually declined from 26 percent to
21.5 percent in the 1960s and 1970s (see Figure 1-1). Similarly, exports
grew faster in many other countries, leading to a smaller share of
world exports for the United States (from 16 percent in 1960 to 11 percent in 1980). Most LDC growth is attributable to OPEC oil exports
(rising from 6 percent to 15 percent). In fact, Japan alone doubled its
share of world trade in this period from 3 to 6 percent, as Figure 1-2
shows. Many other so-called advanced developing countries (the "new
Japans") such as South Korea, Taiwan, Brazil, Singapore, and Indonesia also increased their proportion of world trade.

   Trade remains a smaller proportion of the U.S. economy than that
of its major trading partners, which in part explains differences in outlook on international issues. U.S. government assistance programs,
private investment, and voluntary contributions have helped develop
many countries, but the purchases of the United States, and in recent
years its continued trade deficit, have played an even bigger role.

   While the United States depends increasingly on foreign markets

Figure 1–1.   The U.S. Position in the World Economy is Shrinking.

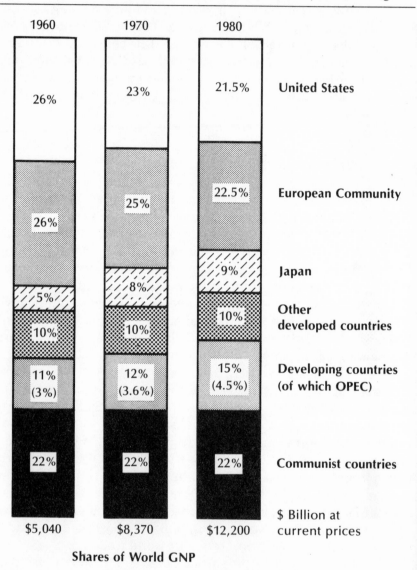

Shares of World GNP

Source: U.S. Department of Commerce (1981).

for growth, the average consumer is relying more on foreign suppliers. The flow of direct investment into and out of the United States is growing and now roughly in balance, even further augmenting the country's "internationalization." As other countries grow faster than

Figure 1–2. The U.S. Position in World Trade is Shrinking.

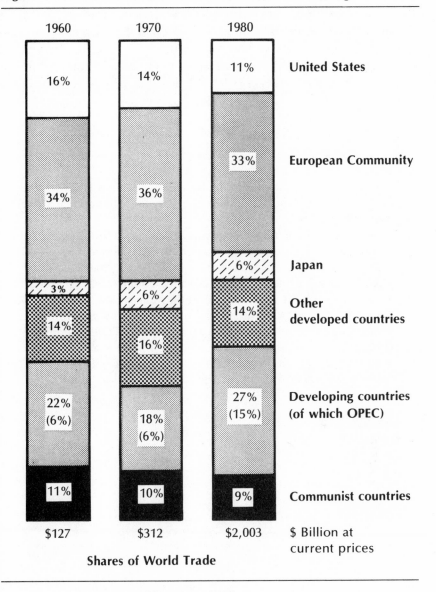

	1960	1970	1980	
United States	16%	14%	11%	
European Community	34%	36%	33%	
Japan	3%	6%	6%	
Other developed countries	14%	16%	14%	
Developing countries (of which OPEC)	22% (6%)	18% (6%)	27% (15%)	
Communist countries	11%	10%	9%	
$ Billion at current prices	$127	$312	$2,003	

Shares of World Trade

Source: U.S. Department of Commerce (1981).

the United States, its relative shares of the world's economy and trade have been decreasing.

Nevertheless, the United States has unmatched economic power in the world, and the dynamism of the U.S. economy continues to astound its critics. Recovering faster, and perhaps more broadly, than the other industrialized countries, its resources, technology, and skills are increasingly devoted to international markets and regaining international competitiveness. The decline in U.S. shares of the world's economy and trade may yet be reversed in the decades ahead, but this will involve coming to terms with the new role of government in the management of international trade.

NOTES

1. A discussion of some of the reasons can be found in Hudgins (1985a).
2. National statistics on trade are compiled by the International Monetary Fund (1983).
3. In 1983 the Western industrial countries accounted for 62 percent of the world's exports. The oil-exporting countries exported 10 percent, the other developing countries exported 14.5 percent, and the rest of the world's exports came from the East bloc trading area, according to a report of the GATT and reported in the Journal of Commerce (1984).
4. Data on U.S. trade have been published in various U.S. Department of Commerce publications, including International Trade Administration (1981, 1984).
5. The effect of overseas investments on U.S. exports is discussed in Stanley, Danielian, and Rosenblatt (1982: 85–91).

II A BRIEF HISTORY

2 THE ORIGINS OF FREE TRADE

Governments have always played a role in international economic affairs. As long as there have been governments and trade between nations, intervention of one sort or another has existed. Governments attempt to achieve stated goals, usually for domestic purposes and with little or no regard to their impact on other countries. The novel characteristic of the present period of international trade is that we preach free trade and nonintervention; but all countries, even the most devout free traders, practice intervention.

Consider briefly some of the early examples of this tension between international trade and government intervention. During the Middle Ages, the limited trade that existed between countries depended on barter — the exchange of goods in the absence of a monetary economy. Toward the end of the fifteenth century, money became common in commercial transactions in southern Europe and spread to northern Europe through the efforts of itinerant traders and money lenders. The discovery and exploration of the New World, the expansion of cities, and the needs of growing states for larger armies and imperial courts all encouraged the new mercantalist system based not on barter but on the acceptance of money to discharge debts.

A new element was introduced into society and dealings between people: The conscious and relentless pursuit of wealth. Mercantilism placed the emphasis of commercial policies on achieving this goal. At the national level, mercantilism translated into the accumulation of wealth in the state or royal coffers. Countries attempted to export the largest possible quantity of their manufactures and import the smallest possible quantity from others, receiving the difference in gold or other precious metals. Governments resorted to all means to achieve this goal, including prohibition of imports, high duties on allowed imports, subsidies and bounties for exports, and restrictions on the export of precious metals. State action was therefore a fundamental principle underlying the mercantilist system.

A parallel development, the international specialization of production, began during the late Middle Ages. For example, Flanders became known throughout Europe for its linens and textiles, Germany for its steel, and Italy for its food products. In some cases international division of labor was actually organized through new enterprises; Hungary, for instance, raised pigs that were fed on imported German grain and exported as hams back to the German market. These trends were later to become part of the doctrinal benefits of free trade (Braudel 1982).

One lasting consequence of these developments was the creation of a sense of national interest associated with economic strength, a concept missing in the Middle Ages. Nations as a whole, and not just individuals, entered into a competitive struggle for wealth. States became interested in the accumulation of wealth through commerce and took steps to encourage or even command the creation of new industries. Production was subjected to regulation designed to ensure quality and value, and thus attractiveness in foreign markets. High duties raised revenue and protected domestic "infant" industries. Colonies and dependencies were restricted to trade with only the parent country. Mercantilism was undoubtedly effective in achieving its objectives.

The mercantilist system was perfected in the sixteenth century in Spain, Italy, France, Holland, and England. In the seventeenth century Holland reaped the greatest benefits as Italy lost its earlier maritime supremacy and Spain and Germany suffered from internal wars and dissention. To contain the growing power of Holland, Britain, under Cromwell, sought ascendancy of the seas and in 1651 passed the Navigation Act. This act restricted trade among British ports and thus between Britain and the colonies, to British ships manned by British seamen. This policy eliminated the Dutch and others from the lucrative trades and was the basis for centuries of British maritime domination. The Navigation Act was also the first modern law of cargo preference, or cargo reservation, and the prominent precursor of a plethora of similar trade and investment restrictions adopted by most countries.

Another important development of the seventeenth century was the directed reformation of the entire French economy under Minister Jean Baptiste Colbert. He tackled the domestic as well as international economies, establishing entire industries and new trading relationships along mercantilist principles in the drive toward industrial growth. Extremely high tariffs protected and encouraged domestic manufacture. New canals, ports, roads, and other public works were undertaken. And the country's public finances were reorganized to improve the fairness and equity (such as it was) of the tax system.

In both Britain and France new forms of production were encouraged through government. The dignity of industry and its national worth were firmly established through mercantilism. By improving industry and enhancing trade, both countries also attracted skilled workers from all over Europe. These technicians brought the latest technology and methods of production with them. When other countries grew concerned about the effect of the skill losses to their own industry, emigration was increasingly prohibited. But the damage was done, and Britain and France benefited by the conscious promotion of industry.

As industry and commerce grew in the seventeenth and eighteenth centuries, the limits of strict mercantilist policies were being reached. Adam Smith contributed to the end of mercantilist theory with his demonstration that gold and silver, the object of mercantilist acquisition, were only commodities like any others. They could be accumulated when demand was sufficient and supply available; but the value placed upon them was one of convention between buyers and sellers. Countries and individuals could also place value on currencies, for example. The mere accumulation of precious metals did not in itself improve standards of living and in fact could become a sterile goal. The real wealth of nations stemmed from their productive capacity and resources, and from their ability to capitalize upon them.

THE ORIGINS OF FREE TRADE

The notion that free trade is superior to protectionism derives from Adam Smith and David Ricardo, two British economists writing in the late eighteenth and early nineteenth centuries. In his pioneering work, Smith assessed the failures of mercantilism. He demonstrated the virtues of a new doctrine, free trade, to guide the relations between countries and traders. The basic economic principle of free trade rests on the concept of the voluntary exchange of goods. The assumption in such an exchange is that each party gains something of greater value than that with which it parts. Since each gains, the general welfare is increased; hence the more trade opportunities that exist, the better. The operations of the market will thus lead to the maximum benefit of individuals as well as of nations, if trade between them is facilitated and unhindered.

Smith concluded that the restrictions placed on trade and the encouragement of it, both features of mercantilism, were at the expense of the general welfare. He recognized that certain actions would be taken regardless of cost — for reasons of defense or of public policy. But as a general rule he argued for the freest possible markets, with neither limitations on private transactions crossing borders nor encouragement of domestic industries through protectionism. Adam Smith is truly the father of free trade in its purest form. The foundation was laid by the publication of Smith's *The Wealth of Nations* in 1776.[1]

Ricardo's contribution was the elaboration of the theory of comparative advantage, which argued that countries should specialize in the products they could most efficiently produce. By the early nineteenth century, Britain was the undisputed leader among the trading nations, and its policies carried international significance — they determined the course of world trade. Some isolated attempts were made during the late eighteenth century to reform trade policy in Britain along the lines proposed by Smith. Negotiations were undertaken between Britain and the United States to allow American vessels and traders access to the lucrative West Indian trade, which was even more valuable than that between the two negotiators. (The trade was so lucrative that Jefferson even urged foreswearing further development of American industry for development of the New World's agriculture to become Britain's grainery.) These negotiations failed in 1783, not because of objections from the newly freed colonies but because British shipowners insisted on retaining their privileges. In spite of this setback, a treaty was successfully concluded between France and Britain in 1786 to relax certain tariffs.

In the first third of the nineteenth century pressures increased within Britain for the removal of barriers to free trade. Britain had outpaced its industrializing rivals: It monopolized world textile and hardware trade, and its ships had access to all of the world's ports while the Navigation Act protected its shipping industry from foreign competition at home. To those in the new and emerging British industries, free trade seemed to offer the greatest rewards. If British hardware was to be sold abroad, then something had to be bought in return. Others, deriving their living from protected industries such as agriculture and shipping, resisted. The Conservatives in 1842 sought to increase trade by export duties and reducing import duties on 750 products, with further reductions in 1845. The conflict came to a head when the divisive issue of agricultural imports arose in parliament.

For decades British farmers had been protected by prohibitive trade barriers known as the Corn Laws (corn being the British word for wheat, the staple crop). The leader of the Conservative party, Sir Robert Peel, had followed the traditional party line in supporting protection. However, when faced with the prospect of potato blight in Ireland and of bad weather in England, which would reduce the harvests and lead to famine, Peel changed his position and proposed importing corn. In a major reversal of British trade policy that opened the doors, in 1846 the protectionist corn laws were repealed.[2] Thus the die was cast and protection of British agriculture was no longer a viable political policy. From this date Britain became the ardent champion of free trade.

However, the new free trade policy was perceived by many outside Britain as excessively self-serving. Throughout the rest of the Victorian era, trade within the expanding British Empire was controlled by strict policies. These policies, set by the British Parliament alone, were designed to protect British manufacturers from foreign competition, to preserve colonial markets for British firms, and to limit the colonies to supplying Britain with raw materials. The classic example was the export of raw cotton from India to Britain for weaving into cloth to be exported back to India. Ghandi attacked these policies, particularly the restriction on raw materials export, in his drive to achieve Indian independence. Only with the passing of the colonial system has this preference for mother country trade been reduced.

The widespread advocacy of the policy of free trade reached its peak in the 1870s. It gained wide acceptance on the Continent, with

Holland most notable for putting the policy into practice. For a comparatively brief period in the 1860s and 1870s, when Europe accounted for about two-thirds of world trade, "the world came close to attaining the ideal conditions postulated by classical economic theory" (Kenwood and Lougheed 1983: 74). But the brief moment passed as other nations rose to challenge British trade supremacy.

THE LEADING PROTECTIONISTS

In the second half of the nineteenth century, there were two new leading trade contenders, the United States and Germany. In contrast to the Adam Smith ideal of a more cosmopolitan world, these two employed protectionism in external trade as conscious tools of national development. In both the United States and Germany, large companies came to dominate manufacturing, in contrast to the more diffuse power structure of Britain. Moreover, these new industrial competitors were becoming eminently successful through protective tariffs and through powerful monopolies, cartels, and trusts.

Protectionism began in the United States with the birth of the nation. With no substantial industry in the new country there had been no organized effort on behalf of manufacturers. In 1791, however, Secretary of the Treasury Hamilton, in his Report on Manufactures, advocated a rigorous program in support of protectionism: levying duties on rival articles; prohibiting outright certain imports; prohibiting export of raw materials for manufacture; offering bounties and premiums to encourage production; instating import exemptions for manufacturing materials; and encouraging inventions.

Following Hamilton's report there was general agreement that developing industry would be desirable. In time almost every one of his proposals was adopted. Adding small duties (the only practicable source of revenues) to the natural barrier of distance and the cost of transportation favored new manufactures. New domestic industry continued the movement of independence from the Old World, as did regulations prohibiting foreign shipping in the coastal U.S. trades.

In contrast, internal U.S. trade was made totally free by the commerce clause of the Constitution, demonstrating the virtues of free exchange and industrial specialization within a large market. As a result it thrived, especially during 1806–1815 when the struggle between

France and Britain interrupted Continental trade. At the close of the War of 1812 with Britain, the United States imposed higher duties on imports, increasing them steadily until 1830 and then leveling them off until the Civil War in 1861. The necessity for revenues to prosecute the war lead to ever higher duties. The end of the war should have reduced these duties, but they were kept high by political actions of industrial interests.

The result was to turn the United States from an agricultural nation into an industrial one at an unprecedented rate. From the outset there was concern about the high cost of domestic labor and raw materials. Duties were urged, not only to provide protection to infant industries but also to encourage or even require the use of domestic supplies and resources. To advocate free international trade was unpatriotic. The shipping and sugar industries were encouraged by bounties; foreign (cheap) labor was excluded; and the home market was reserved for home production. In the name of nationalism, the government developed or subsidized canals and railroads, just as it did for many other projects, programs and reforms. Thus nineteenth century protectionism carried over to the twentieth century, proving its worth and leading to many progressive policies of government.

The tariff policy of the other new contender, Germany, was very similar. The independent German states first had to establish absolute free trade among themselves, just as the thirteen American colonies had done. Then the German states developed political union and eventually political independence. By the time of Bismarck in the 1860s the *Zollverein*, or customs union, was an article of faith among German nationalists and was coupled with protection for domestic industry. Germany experienced the same rapid transformation from an agricultural to an industrial society. By the turn of the century, Germany too had the industrial strength to challenge Britain's international hegemony.

The result of these policies in the latter part of the nineteenth century was extensive bilateralism. It has been estimated that about 70 percent of all trade was bilateral, with trade accounts settled between each pair of trading partners. Only a relatively small part, perhaps 20 to 25 percent was truly multilateral, with the unfavorable trade balance between two countries being settled by a third, which in turn earned a surplus from a fourth (Kenwood and Lougheed 1983: 108). This pattern was to persist until World War I.

THE TWENTIETH CENTURY

Beginning in the 1880s, the search for overseas colonies reached un-precedented proportions. Africa was divided among the European powers; Burma and Malaya were controlled by Britain; Indochina was controlled by France; and the United States began to exert influence in the Philippines and Central America. The need for new markets and new sources of raw materials (particularly tropical products) and the search for new investment opportunities for surplus capital are frequently cited as the economic basis for the scramble. And Germany was the only "great power" without valuable colonies. Thus at the beginning of the twentieth century, the international economic challenge presented by Germany to Britain took the most direct form: war.

With the onset of World War I the capacity of all nations to wage war was increased, as was the state's role in economic affairs. The war intensified protectionism, not only among the combatants, but also elsewhere throughout the trading community. Japan, India, Australia, and some countries in Latin America developed their own industries to replace the lost European exports. After the war these newcomers demanded and received protection for industries such as iron and steel in Australia; iron, steel, textiles, paper, and chemicals in India; and pharmaceuticals in Argentina. The new nations of Europe, carved out of the Austro-Hungarian and Turkish empires, also sought to develop their economic independence through protectionism.

Finally in the immediate postwar period, Britain, France, the United States, and the other victors all raised their tariff levels—the United States to the highest in its history. Currency stabilization, domestic industry rebuilding, and pure retaliatory protectionism were rationales. The difficulty the debtor nations, particularly the defeated Central powers, found in exporting to repay their debts led to the depression of the 1930s.

Before the war, state sectors were small but growing. Under the stimulus of war, all grew rapidly, with government policies designed to force development of industry, especially that related to war.

If the exigencies of war forced most governments to become more involved in economic affairs, the political changes and economic difficulties of the interwar period ensured that this involvement would continue and even intensify. The spread of new political faiths, such as communism and fascism, the powerful stimulus given to economic nationalism by the war, the economic and financial difficulties of the twenties, and the depression of the thirties made it inevitable that the government would play a larger role in the economic life of the nation than formerly (Kenwood and Lougheed 1983: 188).

Nowhere was this tendency more evident than in two newcomers to the international industrial stage, Japan and Russia. In both countries the state forced the pace of industrialization to catch up with the Western competitors. In Russia, even before the revolution, the state dominated every area of commerce. The state owned the mines, the oilfields, transportation, and thousands of factories. Even when not publicly owned, Russian industry depended on tariff barriers, state subsidies, and public support. The Ministry of Trade promoted private trading, regulated prices, and controlled the use of materials and transportation. It had representatives on the boards of private companies. Under the Czars in the last years before World War I, Russia was the successful embodiment of state collective capitalism. While the revolution changed many aspects of Russian life, the structure of trade and the concept of state involvement in the economy was not new.[3]

The distance Japan traveled to enter the modern world was far greater than that traveled by Russia but was traversed in an even shorter period of time.[4] After being sealed off from the rest of the world in the seventeenth century, Japan dramatically signaled its intentions to modernize and develop rapidly by the restoration of the Meiji form of government, which replaced the Shogunate in 1868. Japan then systematically developed and excelled in technology, medicine, business procedures, and administrative reforms.

Most Japanese, seeing the success of the colonial powers, regarded territorial expansion as essential, given the material poverty of the home islands. Japan's initial foray in 1894 against China yielded Korea, Formosa (Taiwan), and Port Arthur (returned to Russia only through the intervention of Russia, Germany, and France). With forced industrialization, the army was doubled and made self-sufficient, allowing the successful 1904 war against Russia to regain Port Arthur and to establish commercial supremacy in Manchuria. In 1914 Japan entered the war solely to acquire Germany's treaty rights in China and to solidify her hold on the previously acquired territories.

Food supplies and export markets were the motivating factors in this expansion, as they were in the later drive toward World War II.

Between 1910 and 1930, for example, Japan's rice imports tripled as the population and standard of living increased without a similar increase in rice production. The only way to pay for the essentials of food and raw materials, oil and iron ore, and every other necessity was to increase textile and manufactured exports. But these products were already facing cut-throat competition and foreign protective barriers. Japanese leaders saw no alternative to territorial expansion as a means of securing the supplies and the markets for itself. Through enormous efforts the country attained war footing. The influence of the army and the navy on the Japanese government ensured no diversion from these national goals would be tolerated.

The interwar years in terms of trade policy can be divided neatly in two by the year 1930. Before that date postwar reconstruction proceeded fitfully in Europe, but led to a boom in the United States. Far from following an isolationist policy in the years after the defeat of the League of Nations, the United States assumed much more responsibility for keeping the world's economy on an even keel. The United States and Britain jointly supplied the global currency needed for trade, a function of the British pound sterling alone until 1914.[5]

The League of Nations convened in 1927 to attempt to solve the problem of the delayed return to free trade. A short-lived slowdown of tariff increases was negotiated, but the force of events soon overtook the efforts of the diplomats. By 1930 these efforts were suspended as ineffectual.

The United States, in spite of its high tariffs continuing under the Fordney–MacCumber Tariff Act of 1922, promoted the expansion of world trade through the inflation of the U.S. money supply. The Federal Reserve system, created before the war, allowed the expansion of credit without printing more money. While insisting that war loans be repaid, the United States made the repayment easier by cheap money and active government interference in the foreign bond market. The dual aims of supporting U.S. industry and keeping the international economy afloat were not inconsistent, and both were achieved by the economic policy in effect through the 1920s.

The problem with this policy surfaced in 1929. Cheap money for foreign borrowers meant cheap money for domestic ones too, and speculation in stocks soared during the 1920s. Margin trading and new investment trusts were the rage of the day until the stock market crash in October and November 1929. The *New York Times* stock market average had fallen from its high of 452 to 224 at the end of the panic. (It was to fall even further in July 1932, to 58, at the depths of the depression.) Economic decline followed the speculative crash, and the depression was underway.

Congress took many measures to fight the depression. The already high U.S. tariffs were increased to prohibitive levels in 1930 by the Smoot-Hawley Tariff Act. Both the National Association of Manufacturers and the American Federation of Labor urged acceptance of the act, while over 200 economists opposed it and wrote in vain to President Hoover to veto the bill. When the tariffs took effect, world trade was devastated. The U.S. depression quickly spread to an already tottering Europe. Austria's leading bank, the Creditanstalt, collapsed the following year, toppled other banks, and forced Britain and other countries off the gold standard. Since the free exchange of gold had been one of the fundamental institutions upon which trade rested, the scarce remaining gold disappeared. U.S. banks in turn began to fail and the depression settled in, not to be relieved until World War II production in the United States and Europe revived industry once again. Nevertheless the high tariffs stayed in place, and to this day the term "Smoot-Hawley" is a rallying cry of free traders everywhere.

Japan was not alone in preparing for war through international trade measures. In Eastern Europe, Germany too had developed both the theoretical need for *Lebensraum*, or living space, and the practical means, a war machine, to achieve it. Germany remained the European country with the greatest potential strength throughout the 1920s even saddled with reparations payments. With the rise to power of Hitler and the Nazis in January 1933, this potential was realized. Industry flourished and state preparation for war implied extensive intervention in the domestic and external economies. The Nazis did not nationalize private industry but left it in private hands willing to carry out the state's directives. Through the stability of government (in contrast to the earlier Weimar period), the inherent strength of the economy, the public works undertaken by Hitler, and the policy of cheap money, by 1936 Germany alone among major countries had regained full employment.

The loss of the gold standard for settling international accounts, U.S. Smoot–Hawley tariffs, and Britain's conversion to protectionism were overwhelming events of the period because of their effect on international trade policy. By the end of the 1930s almost half of the world's trade was restricted by tariffs alone, with even more restricted by quotas, nontariff barriers, and other policies. Eleven countries had adopted licensing quota systems by 1932, which required government approval of every trade transaction. The number grew to twenty-eight (nineteen of them European) by 1939. Clearly world trade had come under substantial government control and free trade was only a vague memory.

The advent of World War II in 1939, as in the First World War, expanded the control of trade by governments. Embargoes were placed on trading with the enemy. War mobilization in every country involved detailed and specific control of strategic imports, allocation of raw materials, control of prices, priority for war production, and financial support for overseas suppliers. All policies were subordinated to the goal of victory. The United States provided war material to Britain and Russia before and after its own entry into the war after Pearl Harbor in December 1941. The mask of neutrality could be dropped once war was declared, and the U.S. war production machine began to turn in earnest. Thus by the end of the war, U.S. industries were operating at full speed, U.S. finances were improving, its trading capacity and shipping were second to none, its major competitors were devastated, and the country embarked on the postwar era with an optimistic attitude.

NOTES

1. For articles written in the earlier inimitable magisterial style of the British economists describing the various elements of mercantilism, free trade, protection, balance of payments and other topics, see the Encyclopaedia Britannica (1910–1911) from which much of this history is derived.
2. In reaction, Benjamin Disraeli and others formed a Protectionist party and defeated Peel's government. Although the harvests were not as bad as expected and the famine did not occur, Peel was exonerated even though he could no longer lead the Conservative government (Maurois 1928).
3. For a wide-ranging and thought-provoking discussion of the impact of the expansion of government in the twentieth century, see Johnson (1983). His discussion of the Russian and Japanese experiences begins on p. 14.
4. Japan's economic problems before both wars are described in Johnson (1983: 176–89).
5. U.S. international policy is discussed in Johnson (1983: 232–33).

3 THE UNITED STATES AND THE GATT

After World War II the United States took the lead in advocating free trade among nations. The postwar planners vowed never again to allow the world to fall victim to uncoordinated economic policies and measures. This was the motivation behind proposals for the United Nations, the World Bank, the International Monetary Fund (IMF), and the stillborn International Trade Organization (ITO). The world community accepted the first three proposals but was unprepared to accede to the disciplines implicit in the ITO proposal. The best that could be done was to create the framework for negotiations between nation states acting independently. That framework was the General Agreement on Tariffs and Trade (GATT). The GATT remains today the only universal international trade agreement, and as such it shapes the international economy in fundamental ways.

The United States negotiated for including in the GATT two essential principles of free trade: reciprocity in commitments and most-favored nation treatment of imports. The United States led the nations in a series of eight tariff negotiations to reduce tariffs to their present level of relative unimportance (at least among most developed countries). This achievement has contributed significantly to the growth of trade and of the free world's economies since the 1940s.[1]

The dictatorial governments of Germany, the USSR, Japan, and Italy used the interwar years and their militant ideologies to bend their economies toward preparation for war. Their drive contrasted sharply with the depression, in which the United States and most other democratic states were mired. The virtual collapse of trade and of the international economy in the 1930s influenced a generation of statesmen who sought at the end of World War II to find ways to integrate economies and legislate prosperity.

After the dark days of the Smoot–Hawley Tariff (enacted in 1930) and after seeing its effect on world trade, the United States explicitly adopted free trade principles to maximize the international welfare. This position was eloquently stated by Secretary of State Cordell Hull in 1937:

> I have never faltered, and I will never falter, in my belief that enduring peace and the welfare of nations are indissolubly connected with friendliness, fairness, equality and the maximum practicable degree of freedom in international trade (Hull 1937: 14).

In a way the industrial and military superiority of the United States at the end of World War II was similar to the dominant position of Britain in the 1880s. Britain too had espoused free trade and sought to maintain an open system in its own interests as well as in the interests of its trading partners. As long as the major trading partners in the developed West could jointly set the rules of trade through the GATT, universal free trade was considered a practicable and attainable goal. The following analysis will focus on the specific institutional and political initiatives to implement this policy.

ORIGINS OF THE GATT

The years immediately following World War II were particularly valuable for laying the foundations of the international economy of the next forty years. The World Bank, the IMF, the United Nations Development Program, and several other international organizations have an impact on trade and investment, but their primary purposes are to promote development and to stabilize the world economy by financing temporary balance of payments difficulties. Their impact on trade has been less direct than that of the paramount trade organization, the General Agreement on Tariffs and Trade.

The GATT emerged as the central international trade institution by default as much as by intention. Most of the diplomats concerned with trade had originally supported the establishment of the International Trade Organization, a quite different body. The United States and Britain agreed upon the proposals for the ITO charter in a series of meetings during the war. The ITO would have been an organization with substantive rules to govern trade and with the authority to enforce them.

The basic U.S. negotiating position in both the ITO and the GATT was simple and unequivocal: Tariffs should be reduced through international negotiations, and all other barriers to trade (nontariff barriers) should be abolished immediately. This position, in its unadulterated form, could not be accepted by the other negotiating nations. Despite pressure from the United States, other countries were unwilling or unable to abandon the protection and controls they had imposed during the war and soon after. Prewar trade had been destroyed not only by the war but also by the loss of colonies, the advent of the cold war that split Europe in two parts, and the postwar inflation. Wealth was concentrated in a few countries, while many teetered on the edge of bankruptcy. The U.S. Marshall Plan had not yet begun to rebuild Europe.

Moreover, there were many diverse views on trade and development issues. These views arose from a country's history, prewar experiences, form of government, and stage of development. The differences hinged on whether a country was firmly committed to market principles or to socialist methods, whether it was developed or developing, and whether it was a member of a trade preference group (such as the former British colonies now participating in the British Commonwealth).

In the absence of agreement on regulating international trade, negotiators supported the International Monetary Fund. The IMF's own policies limited it to supporting currencies only as a last resort. Exchange rate adjustments were expected to bear the brunt of the payments imbalances. Even if the United States had been able to achieve agreement in principle through the ITO to its demands for reductions in tariffs and the elimination of nontariff barriers, few countries would have been able to abide by the agreement in practice.

The most important difference between the United States and other countries centered on the appropriate role of the ITO, as an international organization, in enforcing decisions of its members. This issue is still being debated today. The United States proposed that the ITO enforce a "code of laws" much as a court does. Other countries were not prepared to draft such a code of laws and were especially unwilling to have them enforced by a neutral international body. The solution adopted by the ITO negotiators was to draft broad principles and then temper their force by including loopholes in fine print. The proposed ITO Charter contained so many exceptions and qualifications that *Fortune* magazine editorialized that "[e]very nationalistic trade-control device now in use, and every excuse for using it, is somewhere in this document invoked and permitted" (*Fortune* 1949).

The final charter, drawn up in 1948 in Havana (thus known as the Havana Charter) was not acceptable to the U.S. Senate and could not be ratified. As a result it was not ever submitted to the Senate by the Truman administration. Thus the ITO passed into oblivion, but not before giving new life to the one international agreement regulating trade, the GATT.

THE RISE OF THE GATT

Fortunately for the growth of the international trading system, trade liberalization did not die with the ITO Charter. Many of its substantive provisions had been incorporated in the GATT negotiated in 1947. This agreement has formed the framework for world trade ever since, despite its obvious deficiencies. As then Professor, now Deputy Secretary of State Kenneth Dam put it, "In one of the happiest examples of ingenuity in the history of international organizations, the GATT has risen above the legalistic confines of the text of the General Agreement and has improvised numerous procedures. These procedures have gone a long way toward overcoming the original weaknesses of the U.S. approach" (Dam 1970: 16).

The General Agreement on Tariffs and Trade was in fact the record of a specific tariff negotiation. When it became clear the ITO was not viable the General Agreement became the founding document of a new organization. Since it does not have the organizational or procedural provisions planned for the broader ITO, over the years the GATT has had to operate in a legal limbo. Nevertheless it embodies the most important substantive trade principles proposed by U.S. diplomats.

Today the GATT has ninety members, representing all of the developed countries, many developing countries, and a few socialist countries. It retains the fiction of being an agreement rather than an organization; that is, the decisions are made by the member countries and not by the staff. In the meetings of the contracting parties, the fiction works well, with leadership of the affairs resting on the major trading states, and especially on the United States.

The General Agreement deals primarily with tariffs, but it also affects other areas, such as nontariff barriers, investment, and development. Its greatest importance, however, is not in specific rules but in fundamental assumptions about the international economy—that tariff and trade concessions must be reciprocal bargains and that all nations must be treated equally. These two principles are contained in numerous detailed provisions in the basic GATT and in subsequent agreements, codes, and decisions over the last thirty-five years. They are the key assumptions upon which international trade liberalization rests.

The first of these two principles requires that every nation bind its tariffs so that they cannot be arbitrarily or capriciously increased to protect domestic industries or to harm particular exporters. These agreements are negotiated at tariff conferences. Seven major conferences have been held, most recently the Kennedy Round from 1964 to 1967 and the Tokyo Round from 1975 to 1979. The negotiating countries "trade" tariff concessions, giving and getting tariff reductions on items of interest. No party is required to lower any tariff unless it receives a compensating benefit from another country.

Once agreement is reached, the tariff on that item is "bound" and a country may not raise the tariff without paying a penalty. There are provisions allowing countries to raise the tariff if the concession unexpectedly damages a domestic industry, but then the affected exporting country may also raise its own tariffs. Thus the concept of reciprocal bargains is retained even when expectations are not met.

The GATT offices are in Geneva, in a building that once belonged to the International Labor Organization and still bears the murals dedicated to the dignity of work. There are approximately three hundred employees, all international civil servants from almost every country that is represented by the GATT. These offices contain the large volumes of bound tariff rates agreed on by countries in all previous tariff negotiations.

The "most-favored nation" principle is the cornerstone of the GATT, and thus the international trading system. Article I of the GATT provides that all tariffs, whether or not negotiated through the GATT, and all other rules and formalities of exporting and importing must be applied equally to all other member nations. Discriminatory or capriciously illiberal treatment is outlawed. In this way, no one trading partner has an advantage over any other. The GATT has had to wrestle with many challenges to this principle, but it remains the most fundamental of the concepts governing international trade and investment. Without it there would be even greater anarchy in the world's economy than there is today.

Even this principle was accepted only with exceptions. There were a number of trade "preferences" in existence when the GATT treaty was negotiated, and those benefiting from them insisted that they be preserved. The most widespread was the Commonwealth system of former British colonies, which allowed British goods preferential tariffs in India, Canada, Australia, and several other countries. It also allowed those countries to trade with Britain and with each other with similar advantages. There were also preferential agreements in effect for France, Belgium, and the Netherlands. The United States registered a preferential arrangement with the Philippines.

A more troublesome general exception was carved out for any future customs unions or free trade areas. As with the European Common Market and other similar postwar creations, these unions are inherently discriminatory and therefore violate the most-favored nation principle. The justification for allowing such unions is that they were perceived as steps toward free trade not only for members of the customs union but for other nations as well. This promise has yet to be realized.

The third major exception was not part of the original treaty but was added in the 1960s and reflected the growing international interest in assisting developing countries. The GATT adopted a fourth part to the basic agreement, essentially releasing developing countries from many of the obligations binding developed countries. The developing countries are not required to offer reciprocal concessions in trade negotiations; they can (and therefore expect to) get more than they give. Developed countries are expected to reduce tariffs and other barriers to exports from developing countries faster than they do for other exports. And developed countries are expected to institute "generalized systems of preferences" for exports from developing countries. These provisions recognize in concrete ways the vital importance of exports and trade to the development of all economies, but especially to those of poorer countries.

The question of the enforceability of GATT decisions arose again at the 1982 GATT ministerial meeting, when the members' trade ministers met for the first time in more than a decade to consider the future of the organization. The U.S. delegation had supported efforts to institute in the GATT a more judicial approach to settling disputes between member states (the GATT deals only with intergovernmental problems, not disputes between private traders.) Rapid decisionmaking is essential if the GATT is to remain a valuable source of international rules. In the past it has been hamstrung by lack of mediators, rules, and procedures for settling disputes.

THE GATT'S CONTRIBUTION TO TRADE

The GATT is by no means perfect, even in handling trade matters. There has been considerable criticism in the last few years of its inability to resolve disputes quickly and authoritatively. This shortcoming is directly related to its nonjudicial status as a compact among consenting countries. If the International Trade Organization had been established instead, the situation might be different. The GATT has also been criticized (mostly by the United States, but also by other developed countries) for failing to extend its disciplines beyond trade in commodities and manufactures to trade in agriculture and services.

The GATT's failure adequately to cover agricultural products has been a matter of contention for decades. At the 1982 ministerial meeting, the U.S. delegation forcefully argued for the inclusion of greater discipline in both areas. At a provocative press conference at the Geneva meeting, both Senator Jessie Helms and Senator Robert Dole (senators from farm states and on the Agriculture Committee) warned that the United States would retaliate unilaterally against foreign unfair trade practices in agricultural trade if the GATT did not adopt and enforce better rules governing subsidies for farm exports. The United States has subsequently subsidized farm exports and taken other steps to carry out that threat.

The unwillingness of the GATT contracting parties to accept trade in services as well as trade in merchandise is particularly troublesome. Services have become an increasingly significant but increasingly regulated part of trade. The GATT should define the service industries, understand their contribution to trade, and set guidelines for the permissible national regulation of services trade.

The GATT has made some progress, but not nearly enough, in eliminating nontariff barriers, trade-related investment restrictions, and other barriers to free trade. Tariffs are not the only means of controlling trade, especially in socialist and communist countries, advanced and poorer developing countries, and even some of the most developed countries, such as Japan. Negotiations devoted to these issues have lasted ten years and will have to continue before substantial results are achieved.

The 1982 ministerial meeting is increasingly regarded as a failure. If trade policy does not move ahead with negotiations to liberalize trade, it is seen as a step backward toward protectionism; the status quo is unacceptable. Ambassador William E. Brock, the U.S. trade representative and head of the U.S. delegation, worked with delegations from around the world to achieve meaningful results. Critical meetings were held with leaders of the all-important European Community trading bloc, with leaders of the Third World groups, and with many other delegations.

In these meetings the United States urged acceptance of its work program for the GATT. There was support from a number of different quarters, including the leaders of the free market Southeast Asian countries, the deputy prime minister of Jamaica, several Latin American trade ministers, and the Hungarian trade minister. Resistance came from the organized Third World and from the European Community. The developing countries continued to oppose a greater role for the GATT. The Europeans feared any initiatives that limited their ability to impose import restrictions to protect their industries or to promote their exports, particularly agriculture, through subsidies. A breakthrough on the major issues was never achieved.

The ministerial meeting could only arrive at a "papering over" of differences, without meaningful trade liberalization. Whether its failure will have lasting effects remains to be seen. There are clearly improvements that should be made in the GATT, but international diplomacy takes time. There are indications in 1986, for example, that a new round of trade negotiations may begin to address some of the problems left unsolved at the 1982 ministerial. There are always new steps to be taken.

But the GATT can claim some significant achievements thus far. Much of the expansion of world trade in the year following World War II must be attributed to the GATT's principles of nondiscrimination, trade liberalization, and the GATT-negotiated reduction of tariffs. Consider what the history of U.S. tariffs (paralleled by other industrial countries) has meant for the world's exporters and importers (Cline 1983):

- U.S. tariffs averaged almost 60 percent in 1932 under Smoot–Hawley, and were matched by those of most other trading nations.
- At the end of World War II, in 1946, U.S. tariffs averaged 26.4 percent, but many other countries maintained higher wartime levels.
- After several small tariff-negotiating rounds, U.S. tariffs in 1955 averaged about 12 percent.
- The Dillon Round (1960–62) and the Kennedy Round (1964–67) reduced U.S. tariffs by one-third (to 8 percent).
- The latest round, the Tokyo Round (1973–79), will lead to a U.S. tariff level of 4.3 percent when fully realized in 1987.

By the end of the Tokyo Round's cuts, the rates of the nine European Economic Community nations that took part in the negotiations will range from 5.2 to 6.9 percent. Perhaps even more surprising, given the criticism surrounding its other trade policies, Japan's average tariff rate in 1983 was 2.9 percent, lower than any other major industrial country.[2]

The GATT has achieved one of its major goals: It has essentially completed the task of removing tariffs as a barrier to trade between developed countries. For most products, tariffs are no longer a barrier inhibiting economic activity between industrial countries. While some products and sectors are protected by tariffs considerably higher than the averages quoted, the general trend has been as the original drafters of the GATT had hoped. The economies of the major trading nations have benefited in many ways—from jobs created in exporting industries to greater variety of consumer goods at cheaper prices. The lessons of free trade are clear.

But not every country interprets the results in the same way. Many find inconsistencies with their own domestic political and economic systems. Those that believe in the policy of unrestricted free trade are now few in number. The industries and products that benefit from free trade are being attacked by protectionist pressures from all sides. Those opposed to protection are powerless to prevent it. The political will is wavering even in the United States, free trade's most ardent advocate. The relentless movement toward a different trade system is underway.

Governments have sought to control not only their domestic economies but their external trade and investment relations as well. Although they have benefited from the free trade system, they have also tried to escape its rigors. By influencing the flows of trade and investment through policies and actions, governments already have begun to "manage trade."

NOTES

1. For the authoritative analysis of the GATT and its provision, see Dam (1970) from which much of the early history discussed in this section is derived.
2. Product-by-product negotiations had reached their practical limit in the Dillon Round. The Kennedy Round adopted linear reductions in tariffs on groups of products. Because of their low levels, tariffs are no longer meaningful barriers on a wide variety of products in trade between industrial countries. The Tokyo Round was probably the last time tariff reductions on industrial products could be negotiated. See Kenwood and Lougheed (1983: 289-96).

4 THE EMERGENCE OF MANAGED TRADE

The concept of managed trade does not conform to any of the classical theoretical systems used to describe international trade. It cannot be called free trade, as envisioned by the founders of the GATT, because it does not rely on the free market system of private buyers and sellers. The market will of course continue to play a role, but it will be increasingly restricted in scope by government decisions and actions. These decisions will take many forms and will affect international trade, directly and indirectly, in numerous ways. Governments will act individually and in concert to influence trade in contravention of free trade policies.

The emerging system cannot be considered strictly protectionist. Not all decisions and actions of government will be taken to protect domestic industries, although many will have that intention and effect. Other actions will be taken for better motives, such as preserving the international financial system; preventing the bankruptcy of debtor countries; assisting in economic development; providing stability in North–South relations; and assisting in the transfer of technology. In the name of these objectives, governments are assuming greater responsibility for the international trade system.

Managed trade refers to the direct intervention of a government in trade and investment to better "manage" its own economy as well as the international one. While motives vary, the result of government involvement and activism is the same: Government policies will increasingly control the trade, investment, and other decisions made by business.

This system of governmental control has several features. A basic working definition is that trade management means the conscious control or influencing of international trade by government for governmental purposes. The major elements of this definition can be examined separately:

- "conscious" means the action is taken for its trade effects, even though the action has other effects;
- "control or influencing" focuses on those actions that operate directly on international trade; and
- "for governmental purposes" limits actions to those fulfilling a public policy need

It is hard to generalize meaningfully about the diversity of practices covered. In some cases, government is itself the buyer or seller. In other cases, the government regulates the trade, the products or services, or even the traders. In all cases, governments set the rules of the game. The best way to proceed is by example.

CLASSICAL TRADE MANAGEMENT

The simplest government action that can be taken to control trade is to impose an embargo on exports of certain goods or on certain destinations. The purpose of the embargo may be to deny assistance to an enemy, to keep needed products at home, or to punish a trading partner. The control is unambiguous, and if the government has the will and the ability to enforce its policy, the control is effective.

As long as these actions to restrain trade are predictable and nondiscriminatory, they may be defended for their other effects. The impact on trade is always weighed against other interests. When the United States embargoes sales of computers to the Soviet Union, for example, the interests of national defense clearly outweigh the loss of the export sales.

The reverse is also simple in concept: the limitation of imports from abroad. When imposed to allow domestic industries to supply products formerly bought from abroad, the action is protectionist. If the domestic industry so protected is a new one, the action is often justified as protecting an infant industry and thus aiding the development of the country.

In industrial countries, outright embargoes of imports are relatively rare. The United States embargoes products of endangered species such as whales, elephants, and leopards. Also, countries generally embargo imports of untested or unapproved drugs and products that violate domestic patents. These actions represent the responsibility of government to protect the health and safety of its citizens and the operation of its economy.

The next step beyond an embargo is the imposition of quotas limiting the quantity of imports and sometimes specifying the country of origin for such products. This action is usually taken in the interest of preserving a basic domestic industry from foreign competition. One example of a classic trade restraining action is the limitation of automobiles that may be imported. The imposition of quotas by GATT member nations is intended to be clearly regulated by rules of the GATT that specify conditions and limit the action in time and effect.

Quotas represent protectionism, however, and have acquired a bad reputation. The better way to restrict imports, according to economic theory, is through tariffs. A tariff places a tax or duty on the imported good based on its value. Usually the duty is a percentage of the value, hence the term ad valorem duties. A major advantage of a tariff is the ability to fine-tune the degree of protection and the volume of revenue generated. (It is worth noting in passing that duties have not been a major source of revenues in industrial countries since the introduction of income taxes.) In theory, the adjustment of the rate of duty will provide the optimal measure of protection.

Tariffs place additional costs on importers and consumers, but there is often the option of using alternative sources. Another advantage of tariffs is that they have promoted the negotiation of multinational tariff reduction rounds. Not only can the degree of domestic protection be adjusted but also the degree of access provided to foreign exporters. Theoretically, reducing a ten percent duty to five percent in the importing country will encourage more imports. In a trade negotiation the benefits achieved by increasing exports are balanced by the losses suffered by imports.

Another advantage of quotas and tariffs from the policy perspective is their "transparency." Reading the legislation, the tariff schedule, and the customs regulations will reveal what rates apply. The rules of the game are determinable and known in advance. And when the newly negotiated tariffs are bound in the GATT, they acquire status under international law, giving rise to rights and obligations. Thus if a country is not abiding by its own rules, it can be challenged in its own courts or in the GATT, and compensation can be obtained.

VARIATIONS ON THE CLASSICAL THEME

Another group of government interventions in trade described by economists is nontariff barriers (NTBs). In a broad sense, almost any regulation or policy that results in the exclusion of imports could be considered a nontariff barrier. The GATT's own catalog of NTBs includes a wide range of government measures. Many, but not all, supplement quotas and tariffs imposed at a country's border. Health and safety inspections may be abused, for example, to exclude products or devices otherwise admissible. Government standards for electrical products or agricultural goods may be similarly distorted.

Countries also employ less obvious means to raise barriers to imports. Products may have to be inspected by "independent" institutes or laboratories and given a certificate of approval before being sold on the importing country's market. Such approval can be denied for a variety of reasons. Insurance may be required of imports not required of domestic products. The government may buy only domestic products, even if the imports are better or cheaper; this barrier is especially important for those industries such as telecommunications, electronics, computers, aircraft, and defense for which the government is the largest or sole customer. Taxes other than duties can be placed on foreign products or sellers.

The GATT members recognize the importance of developing international rules to deal with these nontariff barriers to trade. The approach taken in the 1947 General Agreement was to demand their immediate abolition and to prohibit new ones. Specific provisions of the agreement deal with the NTBs known at the time. For example, they prohibit discriminatory taxes placed on imports and customs examination fees that exceed cost. They also require that laws and regulations concerning imports be published promptly and that antidumping and countervailing duties be applied only in stated circumstances to achieve approved objectives.

In spite of these commitments, countries have nonetheless maintained NTBs. The GATT provides a mechanism for dealing with complaints. But attempts during the Kennedy Round of tariff negotiations to reduce NTBs were unsuccessful. The Tokyo Round concluded a number of specific codes to regulate NTBs, the most important of which dealt with customs inspection practices, government-imposed standards, government procurement, and agricultural standards. Unfortunately, these codes have fewer adherents than the GATT itself and only recently have taken effect, at the conclusion of the negotiations in 1979.

It is premature to speculate on the impact these codes will have on trade. The early returns on the government procurement code's effects are not encouraging; very few U.S. companies reported sales to foreign government markets that had supposedly opened up. The other procedural codes may have improved the prospects of exporters, but their effect is marginal and is certainly of secondary importance to more basic economic forces and the effects of tariff and quota reductions themselves.

All of these classical trade measures are inherent in the sovereign power of each country; they do not result from international negotiations. Diplomacy may advocate their removal, but the decision to change a tariff, a quota, or a nontariff barrier is the independent act of each country.

EXPORTING ASSISTANCE

As the spread of industry, technology, and management has lead to an increasing number of potential exporters in the world, the competition between them has become more intense. Just as a fledgling company may have to "buy into" a few contracts to get business, new exporting nations may have to help their companies. Even established exporters develop exporting assistance programs to meet the competition and thereby preserve their markets abroad.

The most prevalent form of exporting assistance is financial—the provision of tax incentives and low-interest loans to finance overseas sales. This is not to say that sales would not be made without such assistance. But it is clearly an example of government involvement that interferes with the free market. As many would argue, any form of assistance that encourages the devotion of resources to uneconomic projects is either unnecessary, or distortive of market allocation, or both. Nevertheless, governments persist in subsidizing exports in the name of economic development and protecting employment.

And as long as one's competitors do it, the free market arguments are lost.

Other forms of exporting assistance are less troublesome since they do not have the same effect of misallocating resources: Almost all governments supply information and assistance to their exporters regarding markets abroad, trade and economic conditions, and potential customers. Many governments organize trade and investment missions to foreign countries to promote their products and attract new business. Some encourage their producers to form exporting cartels to eliminate competition between them. And a few governments finance the development of new products and technologies in order to win export markets.

The premier example of a country using all of these tools and more to promote exports is Japan. The role of its Ministry of International Trade and Industry (MITI) is justly famed worldwide for its deep involvement in Japan's external trade. Not only does Japan promote exports more aggressively than any other country but until recently it was also the shrewdest exponent of protectionism, skirting the edges of the GATT to ensure that no imports were allowed into Japan until it was ready for them. Japan's management of external trade is very significant to the development of the "new Japans" (the more advanced developing countries) and to the debate on industrial policy in the United States. As the second most advanced economy in the West, Japan's impact will be enormous in the years to come.

Another major way governments promote their exports is through the demands of countertrade and barter. In its simplest form, countertrade means that the seller must take back goods instead of money from the buyer. There are many variations on this theme, but the underlying principle remains the same. Today, a growing number of countries rely on countertrade to balance their trade and to force exports. It is estimated that about 25 to 30 percent of all world trade is bartered, in one form or another, and the proportion will continue to grow.

Countries are forced to countertrade for a variety of reasons. They may be unable to finance a purchase for lack of the foreign exchange. They may be unable to dispose of their own goods on international markets, and therefore they force the foreign seller to do it for them. They may wish to monitor their trade to achieve balances between imports and exports, thus saving scarce foreign currency. Or, they may combine barter with their industrial development plans, forcing foreign investors to buy back the product before allowing them to invest. This last reason is the most alarming development leading to trade management, as it puts government squarely in the middle of previously private market transactions.

BILATERAL DEALS

Another way trade can be managed is through bilateral negotiations between two countries. Instead of raising its own tariffs against an offending import, the concerned country may negotiate with the exporting country for it to control its own exports. These negotiations may yield an agreement between the countries that restricts the export of certain products for a specified time.

These agreements, called orderly marketing agreements (OMAs), theoretically bind the parties to observe the agreement and provide for retaliation if broken. They are commonplace in international trade and help to regulate it. They are a major, but little understood, feature of managed trade.

Alternatively, the exporting country may "voluntarily" restrict its own exports. Of course the degree of voluntariness often depends on the threat of something worse happening if it does not take the action itself. Since there is no formal agreement between the countries, no provisions for adherence or retaliation are included. It is only the continuation of the threat that forces acceptance by the export-controlling country.

The Japanese government agreed in 1981 to voluntarily control exports of Japanese automobiles to the United States. If it had not acted, there was a great likelihood that Congress would have enacted a numerical quota. There was considerable precedent in Europe for such quotas, which protect the automobile industries of France, Italy, and the United Kingdom from excessive Japanese imports. The United States government pressed the Japanese to act in its own self-interest to avoid the passage of legislation in Congress which would be much harder to modify or eliminate when circumstances warranted. The Japanese government agreed and voluntarily imposed the controls.

FREE TRADE AREAS

The reverse of these trade-restraining deals are the preferential trade-encouraging deals in which two or more countries agree to open up their markets to each other on better terms than they give to others. Such deals are consistent with the GATT under its provisions for free trade areas and customs unions (see Chapter 6). One of the first such agreements was negotiated between Belgium, Holland, and Luxembourg to establish a free trade area among themselves. This area was a precursor of the European Common Market, the Latin American Free Trade Area, the Association of South East Asian Nations, and others. The United States and Canada established a limited union for trade in automobiles and automotive parts by treaty in 1963 and are now considering adding other sectors. The affected trade can be limited to specific products, or it can be general.

There is no doubt that such arrangements benefit the participants. They have access to larger markets, they can achieve economies of scale, and they can specialize in their own production—concentrating on those products for which they have a comparative advantage. Such arrangements are nevertheless inherently discriminatory, shutting out products from other countries. If they were truly steps toward larger free trade areas (perhaps encompassing all or most of the GATT members, for instance) then the short-run disadvantages could be overlooked. But these free trade blocs become institutionalized. Trade relationships within the bloc become redirected away from external trade toward internal bloc trade. The chances of expansion are diminished.

Perhaps the most extreme example of the development of this practice is the Soviet Union's East European bloc, the COMECON group. Not only does this bloc trade among itself on preferential terms but it also plans the division of production within the bloc. Such international planning is possible only from centrally planned economies found in the East bloc communist countries. Even there it has not been effective in controlling all trade or in developing the East bloc economies. Nevertheless it represents conscious management of a majority of these countries' trade, and thus a substantial portion of world trade.

The most important way the communist countries manage trade is through state ownership and control of production. Their trade is not open to market forces but subject to the annual and five-year plans. The rigidities and problems of this type of management inhibit trade. There is no other trade except that managed by the government or through government-owned entities.

SECTOR AGREEMENTS

Bilateral or multilateral agreements also cover important sectors of trade such as textiles, automobiles, steel, electronic components, agricultural products, and much more. In some cases the agreements are negotiated solely between governments. They may be either trade-restricting or trade-promoting. In other cases the affected buyers and sellers may agree to the conditions of trade and then have their understandings ratified by their governments.

In still other cases the process may be more confused. The participants in the agreement may include private firms, public entities, cooperatives, or semiautonomous government agencies. Despite this disparity, the result is always some limitation on the scope of private decisionmaking and the opportunities for those outside the arrangement.

Market or trade "stabilization" is usually the purpose of such agreements. In U.S. antitrust law, such agreements would be called cartels, which are illegal. Participants would be subject to fine or imprisonment. On the international stage, even if the United States is a participant, no penalties are assessed. On the contrary, penalties are only assessed if the participant fails to abide by the cartel agreement. Thus free market forces do not and cannot operate in these stabilized trades.

But the cartel only works if it includes all, or substantially all, of the producers. If there are some major suppliers who refuse to participate, then the cartel is weakened accordingly. The OPEC cartel's grip on the oil market of the mid 1970s has weakened substantially with the discovery of oil in the North Sea and in the Alaskan North Slope, and with the widespread development of oilfields in many non-OPEC developing countries. Other arrangements, much less well known, continue to control trade in a wide variety of commodities such as sugar, tin, jute, coffee, and cocoa. These are all attempts of countries to manage the trade of products on which their economies depend. Obviously the realities of getting good prices for their production take precedence over theories of free trade.

Producer cartels are not the only market stabilization agreements. There are also arrangements between governments of buyers and sellers to preserve orderly markets. The purposes are varied, but generally the tradeoff proposed is continued access to the buyer's market in exchange for restraints placed on the seller's products. The restraints can be placed by the exporter or the importer, and usually refer to quotas.

The most widespread of these is the Multi-Fiber Arrangement (MFA) controlling trade in apparel. This arrangement allows importing countries to set quotas, by product, for each exporter country. Thus, for example, the United States has a limit on the number of sweaters to be imported from China. The critical point is that this quota is negotiated with and agreed to by China. Furthermore, under the MFA, the exporter bears part of the responsibility for enforcing the arrangement; quite different from ordinary quotas.

Sector agreements are, with the exception of the MFA, negotiated outside the GATT. Even the MFA is handled separately from other GATT undertakings. It is the result of political pressures both in importing countries attempting to preserve what is left of their apparel industries and in exporting developing countries that see apparel production as one of the few industries open to them. This is the reality of international trade as it is managed today.

The problem facing private traders is that they will increasingly be forced to go along with these trends in order to do any business at all. Not only will exports be subject to government import controls but trade will need to conform to the outlines of government agreements. In recent years, about one-third of U.S. markets for manufactured goods have been covered by voluntary quotas and other quantitative restrictions; the levels in other developed countries are similar (Cline 1983). Although commercial diplomacy should come to reflect the realities of business, there is no guarantee that economic considerations will not be subordinated to other concerns. In fact, this is the real problem with trade managed by governments: that it will become trade managed for political, national security, developmental, or other reasons. Economic efficiency and thus the general welfare will suffer as a consequence.

III TRADE MANAGEMENT TODAY

5 TARGETING AND THE JAPANESE MODEL

There has been no shortage of books and conferences in the last fifteen years devoted to the subject of Japan. This book will not go over well-plowed ground to describe the postwar Japanese industrial miracle, their theories of management, or the future of Japanese industrial competition for the United States. It will focus instead on one element of the picture — the role of Japan's government agencies in the management of trade.

The importance of that role cannot be overstated. Japan's success has now been proven beyond doubt. Industrial policy advocates in the United States argue that what worked there could work here. Others doubt the role of the Japanese government in creating the economic miracle, but they do not doubt that its external trade policies have determined its international trade successes. To these observers, the Japanese experience is one to be studied and emulated.

The message from Japan to the advanced developing countries of the world is clear — follow our policies and you too can reach a high standard of living. This means more and more countries will be following Japan's policies. The open, free trade system will be under pressure as never before. That is the challenge of the future.

ORIGINS OF GOVERNMENT INTERVENTION

The Meiji Restoration of 1868 began a systematic and singleminded drive to acquire Western ways and to industrialize. During the period before World War I, Japan built an industrial base. In the interwar period Japan found for the first time that international trade was a necessity for its very existence and set out literally to conquer markets. Its wartime aims were to secure raw material sources and populous markets for its products and to displace the European powers in Asia. For Japan, the Second World War was a desperate lunge that proved unsustainable against the productive power of the United States. Japan's loss prompted the country to redirect its considerable energies and talents into the new drive for economic growth and industrial supremacy in world markets (see Johnson 1983).

The Japanese government has played an extremely important and unique role in this process. Japan has not attempted to nationalize the private sector; private firms have been separate and distinct throughout the hundred or more years of Japan's amazing growth. It did not follow Mussolini and Hitler into a theory of the corporate state embodied in fascism and national socialism. Instead it fashioned with its own tools a way of organizing private enterprise and initiative to serve the ends of the state. The most visible expression of that organization has been the Ministry of International Trade and Industry (MITI) and its several predecessors.

During the Meiji era there was a concerted effort of government bureaucrats to develop the best industries to serve the needs of a modern army and navy — the heavy industries of engineering, mining, and shipbuilding. A predecessor of MITI, the Ministry of Commerce and Agriculture, set out to promote these strategic industries. The ministry originated in 1888 and quickly bent foreign trade to the service of developing the industries targeted. Thus the outlines of Japan's industrial policy took shape a century ago.

MITI AND INDUSTRIAL POLICY

The next phase in the evolution of the present-day MITI was the creation in 1925 of the Ministry of Commerce and Industry. In the 1920s, the ministry saw the end of the boom following World War I, marked by a long recession, the growth of industrial conglomerates, known as the *zaibatsu*, and the declining markets for Japan's exports. As a result of analyses and studies, in 1925 the ministry sponsored two new laws that reflected the change of Japan's industrial policies to the new economic conditions. The first was the Exporters Association law, which allowed and helped create export unions, along specific product lines, among smaller companies. The second was the Major Export Industries Association Law, which restrained competition by organizing cartel-like associations in which firms agreed to share markets and limit production.

The two new laws were controversial and opposed by the *zaibatsu*. They signified a commitment to exports over domestic competition, which has characterized much of Japanese trade policy to date. And they reflected a belief that small firms, if organized properly, could help alleviate trade deficits. A similar theory can also be found in much of the recent U.S. concern and support for small firms. But in the United States as in Japan, the big companies tend to increase their power and control.

In 1927 the ministry tried to clip the wings of the major companies by creating a Commerce and Industry Deliberation Council to discuss industrial policy. The council included representatives for large and small firms, academia, unions, other ministries, local government, new media, and consumers. The most important innovation of the council was the idea that the ministry should orchestrate industrial mergers to eliminate excessive competition. In addition, it was proposed that the ministry increase loans to small companies and export subsidy programs. These programs and others became part of a policy of Industrial Rationalization that continues to inspire MITI's policies today (Schlossstein 1984).

The elements of Industrial Rationalization can be envisioned in four levels. The first level refers to the improvement of enterprises through better production techniques, quality control, and management controls. The second level encompasses the improvement of the environment within which firms operate, including transportation and industrial location. The third is the industry level, which creates the framework for firms to compete or to cooperate in cartel-like arrangements, as appropriate. The last level is the industrial structure itself, which maximizes the opportunities for export success and for meeting international competition.

The ministry institutionalized these policies in the Temporary Industrial Rationality Bureau in the early 1930s. The bureau planned for the control of enterprises, improvements in industrial financing, and production subsidies in key industries. The model for the program was German Industrial Rationalization, occurring along the same lines. The guiding spirit behind this development, Yoshino Shinji, became vice minister because of his success in implementing this policy. He sought to combine a plan for industrial development with government control to eliminate the worst abuses of unbridled capitalism. In doing so he can be considered the father of industrial policy.

The next major step was the Important Industries Control Law of 1931, which allowed two-thirds of the members of an industry to petition the ministry for a cartel. The ministry would approve not only the formation of the cartel but also the way it operated. The members had to ask for approval of member investments, as well as production targets or cutbacks. Periodic reports were required. This law embodied the embryonic licensing and approval by authorities later evident in the term "administrative guidance." Soon after this law was passed, Japan began its conquest of Manchuria. Through the rest of the 1930s all branches of the Japanese government, including the ministry (and thus industry), were subordinate to the military.

During the war the Ministry of Commerce and Industry was renamed the Ministry of Munitions, which supported the war machine and its large suppliers. The bureaucracy continued planning and approving, but now focused on strategic military industries as well as strategic export industries. One interesting indicator of this continuity of theory and policy is the fact that all of MITI's vice ministers during the 1950s had entered its predecessor between 1929 and 1934, the most creative period in the development of industrial policies. They were able to draw from the successes and failures of the prewar period in guiding the postwar miracle.

MITI AND THE POSTWAR ECONOMIC MIRACLE

The Ministry of International Trade and Industry was reborn in 1949 with a broad and powerful charter. It has the responsibility for shaping the structure of industry, guiding industrial production and development, directing foreign trade and commercial relations with other countries, ensuring adequate supplies of raw materials, and managing small business, patents, and technology. The measures MITI takes to discharge these responsibilities fall into three groups:

- protecting the home market and infant industries
- nurturing and developing new industries, and
- intervening to control or "guide" industry through administrative guidance

The first group involves tariffs, nontariff barriers, import controls, foreign exchange controls, and limits on foreign investment. Many of these were extensively used during the early postwar period, but are no longer obviously or blatantly discriminatory in their effect. The next section will examine in more detail the evolution of these protective actions.

The second group involves low-interest loans to targeted industries, special depreciation rules, subsidies, research and development funding, cartels, and foreign technology licensing assistance. The impact of these special aids on trade only recently is becoming better understood, and is fueling U.S. efforts to compensate its industries suffering from competition with such supported industries. This is a prime example of managed exports deserving closer attention.

The third group is primarily internal or domestic in impact, but can also affect international competitiveness. It involves the licensing of plant and equipment investments, supporting cooperative research programs with government funds, and withholding government licensing for activities inconsistent with MITI's plans. For these purposes MITI has access to the government's Fiscal Investment Loan Program, an off-budget fund administered by the Ministry of Finance from citizens' savings in postal savings accounts and national pensions. About half of these funds are invested in the Japan Development Bank, created in 1951 to give long-term, low-interest loans to targeted industries. Other funds are invested in the Japan Export-Import Bank to finance exports or in public investments and local governments. All of these investments are expected to pay the interest on the savings accounts and support the pensions. This is one of the mechanisms by which Japan uses its extraordinarily high savings to meet the needs of the country as seen by MITI.

The last stroke of this broadbrush picture of Japanese industrial policy as it applies to trade management is a law passed in 1978, the Structurally Depressed Industries Law. This law has been used to exclude from Japan imports of those industries considered to be on their way out or overbuilt in Japan, such as aluminum, pulp for paper-making, and certain petrochemicals. The purpose is to give declining industries "breathing room" to adjust to lower levels of demand. Similar laws exist in other countries, but the distinguishing feature of Japanese practice is the administrative discretion given to MITI to use the law as it sees fit. Such discretion differs from that found in most other developed countries, and is yet another weapon in Japan's battle to manage its trade.

MITI is quite open about its plans for the future of Japan. It has issued a series of white papers outlining proposed government policies, and the assumptions on which they are based. In 1971 it issued the report "Trade and Industrial Policy for the 1970s." Four years later MITI published "Japan's Industrial Policy: A Long-Range Vision." The most recent, issued in 1980, is "MITI's Vision of International Trade and Industry Policies for the 1980s." This last document explicitly targeted industries such as computers, information technology, aircraft engineering, and biotechnology for future growth and government support. These are industries in which future competition will be greatest.

THE U.S. RESPONSE TO MITI

In contrast to the all-important role of MITI, the U.S. response reflects a trade bureaucracy that is often ineffective and cumbersome. The Office of the Special Trade Representative (as it was then called) was originally established in the early 1960s to handle the Kennedy Round of tariff negotiations. It had a small staff and discharged its duties; many thought it would be disbanded after the negotiations. Instead, Congress institutionalized the function of trade negotiation outside of the "suspect" State Department, where foreign interests might be taken into account to an excessive degree.

Today, after successive administrations have built up its role, the Office of the U.S. Trade Representative has a staff of 150 (with more borrowed from other agencies), a permanent Ambassador to the GATT in Geneva, and all of the permanence of any other government agency. The U.S. trade representative (USTR) has the role of negotiator even when there are no GATT tariff negotiations in progress, handling the day-to-day business of trade agreements. He advises the president on trade policy, coordinates administration trade and investment policy, and serves as a trade ombudsman for the business community.

The other U.S. government departments concerned with trade and investment policy are Commerce, Treasury, State, Agriculture, Defense, Energy, and Labor. But every other department has international programs of some kind. The coordination job is, of course, a difficult one. The Commerce Department has the largest staff devoted to trade matters (approximately 2000 total in the International Trade Administration). President Reagan and several senators and members of Congress have proposed consolidating it with the Office of the USTR into a new Department of International Trade, absorbing trade policy, promotion and support functions, and agencies from elsewhere in the executive branch. If the proposed department is enacted, the institutionalization of trade management will have taken a great step. Even without the new department, the U.S. government has irreversibly involved itself in the trade management business, but in a much weaker form than its Japanese competitor.

JAPANESE IMPORT MANAGEMENT

Import protection is important not only for industries just getting started but also for declining industries attempting to adjust to new circumstances. In both cases the theory of protection is the same: domestic producers should be protected from competition (especially that from abroad) when they are most vulnerable. In this way the structure of Japanese industry can be changed to improve competitiveness or to deal with new, lower cost industries overseas.

Not only are firms and industries protected but time is allowed for them to develop new products for the home market before mounting export drives. More research and development funding can be derived from government and private sources because of the assurance that the 120 million-person domestic market and the huge internal industrial market can be developed by Japanese firms before foreign competition is permitted. Obviously the foreign firms, when finally allowed to sell, find the entrenched domestic firms hard to surpass.

Such protectionism was a firm policy during the 1950s and 1960s. Tariffs were high; agriculture was protected; quantitative quotas on numerous imports were established; nontariff barriers of great variety and ingenuity were imposed; government purchasing at all levels was closed to foreign bidders; foreign investment in many specific industries was prohibited; and foreign exchange remittances were strictly controlled. The system was complete; it blocked all imports except those forming part of the industrial strategy.

Japan used this policy wisely to assist industries with export potential. Machinery and products were allowed in for the explicit purposes of duplicating or improving them. The first Japanese cameras were copies of German, U.S. and other foreign cameras, but copies selling at lower cost because of lower labor rates. Before long the industry began to develop the marvelously sophisticated products of today, unmatched anywhere in either cost or quality. Japan's camera industry no longer requires protection, no longer benefits from low labor costs, and currently develops and serves markets around the world, based on world-scale production facilities.

In the 1950s textiles and apparel accounted for about one-third of Japan's exports. Only 14 percent was in machinery and equipment. By the mid 1960s machinery and equipment had risen to 40 percent, with metals (e.g., steel) and metal products following at 26 percent. Fibers and textiles had declined to less than 10 percent. Not only was Japan getting out of the declining textile sector but it was aggressively moving into the sectors that it was to dominate for the next twenty years.

This history has been repeated in industry after industry, wherever the conditions have been right. Textiles, steel, shipbuilding, automobiles, and electronics have all followed the same basic pattern — infant protection building up domestic, and then world-scale production. This is also the history that the "new Japans" would like to duplicate. They have not only the precedent but the will to do so. The "new Japans", or newly industrialized countries, have followed the example of Japan, capitalizing on their lower labor rates, their modern plants, and their efficient traders to exploit markets around the world. Only then are import tariffs reduced.

Japan agreed to substantial reductions in its tariffs in the Kennedy and Tokyo rounds of tariff negotiations. Japanese officials can now argue that their tariffs are among the lowest in the world, and that no tariff barriers stand in the way of exporting to Japan. Failures to penetrate the Japanese market are, they say, a consequence of the exporters' lack of perseverance, compounded by unfamiliarity with the Japanese language and culture. These reasons are undoubtedly true in some cases, especially for exporters who have not made the commitment of resources needed to crack the Japanese market.

But these reasons do not apply in other cases where the exporter has made the commitment, has devoted the resources, has succeeded in other foreign markets and still cannot sell in Japan. What conclusions can be drawn from such cases? The most plausible explanation is that nontariff barriers still restrict access, allowing competition only on the terms, conditions, and in the quantities desired by the Japanese.

The elimination of many of these nontariff barriers has required government-to-government negotiations. The United States pressed Japan to set up in 1979 the joint Trade Facilitation Committee. The committee met on numerous occasions in Tokyo and Washington with ranking officials of MITI to find solutions to exporters' particular problems. The problems ranged from the inspection of cosmetics at the border, to the certification of food ingredients by the Japanese Ministry of Agriculture, to the standardization of computer communications protocols.

Over the course of two years of effort the United States negotiated relief from nontariff barriers in 16 of the 21 cases presented. The virtue of this approach for the Japanese lay in its low level of contentiousness; it did not challenge their decisions directly but drew them into a process of jointly seeking solutions to common problems. Only in the most exaggerated cases of delay and obstruction by the Japanese officials did the U.S. negotiators threaten to use public pressure or other tactics to achieve results.

While pursuing this case-by-case method at one level, the United States was also challenging Japan's nontariff barriers at several other levels. In the U.S.–Japan Trade Policy talks, the United States pressed for the elimination of the remaining quotas, particularly those on beef and citrus products. These quotas were instituted after World War II, as protection for the predominantly conservative farmers who were and remain the primary support of the Liberal Democratic Party (in office for the last 40 years). These quotas have been increased over the years, but they remain a symbol of the early protectionist period.

Another effort was made in the Trade Policy talks to deal with systematic nontariff barriers—those used to protect declining industries. The U.S. Department of Commerce organized U.S. exporters of soda ash (a basic industrial commodity chemical used in the manufacture of glass, and in other processes). Imports of soda ash had been shut out of Japan. The Japanese domestic producers had formed a cartel, had limited their domestic production, and were keeping out foreign supplies. Their cost of production was almost double the cost of the U.S. product on the docks in Japan. Obviously this was not a free market. The device used to exclude the U.S. product was nothing as crude as a tariff or a quota. Rather, it was the limitation placed on the ownership of the only loading and unloading facility in Japan capable of handling imports. That facility was owned by the cartel, and the Japanese government would allow no others!

U.S. automobile companies have much to answer for in allowing the Japanese market to slip out of their hands. In the immediate postwar years during the U.S. occupation, U.S. companies of all kinds had a golden opportunity to establish themselves in Japan. U.S. automakers were already well established in Europe and the British Commonwealth countries, and they had the resources to succeed again. Their failure to capture more than a very small part of the luxury car market in Japan deserves more analysis than can be provided here. But one aspect of current Japanese practice is particularly noteworthy. U.S. cars exported to Japan are inspected at the docks not only for safety or mechanical aspects but also for their paint finishes. Those determined to be below Japanese standards must be repainted — surely a curious use of customs inspection to impose an import barrier.

American machine tool producers have complained for years that their products are not allowed into Japan until the domestic producers in Japan are capable of producing an identical or similar machine. Those machines allowed into the market often are admitted only for demonstration purposes and then copied by Japanese manufacturers. With the protected domestic market, the Japanese companies can develop their technology unhindered by foreign competition. Today those companies have superior products and are capturing large shares of the U.S. and European markets. The amount of government help they have received will be described in a later section. Once again, government management of imports assisted the development of a key industry.

BASEBALL BATS AND TRADE POLICY

One of the recent examples of Japanese trade management would be extremely humorous if it did not represent so clearly the difficulties of exporting to Japan. An American manufacturer tried for two years without success to export aluminum baseball bats of the type used by softball leagues in Japan. His efforts were met with a series of rebuffs. First he was told domestic production was sufficient. When that excuse could no longer be supported, he was told that U.S. bats could not be imported unless they were certified, and bats could only be certified in Japan!

Since no bats were allowed into Japan, none could be tested and certified. No league would use an uncertified bat, for fear of losing its insurance in case of injury. Horrific stories were told of bats flying apart and injuring players and spectators. Finally, the United States brought the case to the GATT, as an example of the lengths to which countries would go to exclude imports. The compromise solution, reached through government efforts, allows for certification in the United States.

The baseball bat result is intellectually unsatisfying, but typical of the practical accommodations made in the trade arena. It is precisely this kind of government-negotiated, case-by-case approach that will increasingly characterize the trade-managed world. There will be fewer and fewer "global" solutions to trade problems, and more and more specific, product- or sector-oriented solutions. Governments will spend precious time and energy dealing with the minutiae of trade, not with universal or systemic solutions.

In a sense, both sides will win short-term victories at the expense of the long-term war against protectionism. Countries imposing non-tariff barriers will delay the entry of competing products. This will provide the needed breathing space for new industries, for declining industries in the process of adapting, and for new products establishing themselves in home markets. The exporting country will devote its resources to eliminating the barrier, and in many cases will eventually be successful. The exporter will be able to tackle the market without government hindrance, but only after the negotiations between governments have determined the rules of the game (i.e., U.S. bat certification is acceptable).

The questions remain: For how many products over how many years will this approach need to be followed before the Japanese and other protected markets will truly be open? Are there general solutions that can be negotiated, or must every case be dealt with individually? Will a new round of negotiations in the GATT solve this problem, or at least begin the process? One can hope the trading nations of the world can make that beginning.

EXPORT MANAGEMENT

Consider now the other side of Japan's trade management policy, exporting. The thrust to increase exports is now an article of faith throughout the world. Few countries do not promote their exports, in one way or another. The GATT has provided some guidelines and discipline for its members on what is permissible in supporting exports. Subsidies, for example, are to be avoided. But even basic GATT provisions are in dispute, and their exact limits are not known. This leads to complaints by one member against another that must be resolved through GATT processes.

As the review of its history has shown, early in the Meiji period, Japan began to focus efforts on exporting to survive. MITI has been the preeminent instrument of policy, using a variety of tools to direct and assist exporting industries. MITI has identified promising export industries, provided help, and kept out competition. The exporters work closely with MITI, knowing their cooperation will be rewarded.

In many key industries the cooperation has been so close that MITI can claim much of the credit for Japan's industrial success. In machine tools, steel, textiles, shipbuilding, and heavy construction equipment, the collaboration succeeded. Other industries, such as electronics and automobiles, developed with less direct help. In all cases MITI provided administrative guidance, and its objective was clear—to increase the world market share of Japanese industries wherever possible.[1]

Government assistance takes many forms. At the earliest stages of research, funding goes to approved research ventures. Product development is aided with an eye to foreign markets. Export market surveys and research are provided. Export financing comes from government sources. And government defends the marketing strategies and penetration when it becomes a matter of negotiation between governments.

An example will illustrate the process and the effect of these various measures. Examining the assistance given to the machine tool industry is informative because of the public documentation and the extensive research available, but any of several other industries have the same pattern.

The Japanese tool industry was challenged in a case brought under an obscure provision of U.S. tax law. That provision denies investment tax credit for purchase of foreign-made equipment unfairly subsidized. It was claimed by the U.S. company Houdaille Industries that all Japanese machine tools had received so much help that U.S. law should deny tax credits.

The government review essentially confirmed the evidence presented in the complaint. Over the course of thirty years, Japan took its fragmented machine tool industry and turned it into a cartelized oligopoly composed of a few highly successful manufacturers. Following the pattern already described, MITI used its authority to prepare a basic rationalization plan for the industry. Specific laws were adopted to allow targeting on this industry: in 1956, the law for Promotion of Machine Industry; in 1972, laws for Promotion of Specific Electronic Industry and Specific Machinery Industry, and for Promotion of Specific Machinery and Information Industries. Under these laws MITI instructed industries to decide what products to manufacture, to set production quotas, to restrict technology, and to jointly purchase parts and materials. Mergers were encouraged. The laws specifically fostered anticompetitive behavior and protected it from investigation by the Japanese antitrust authorities.

The machine tool industry could also take advantage of the Export and Import Trading Law, which authorizes various cartel arrangements for exports. Exporters may agree on price, quantity, quality, and design of export products, and on domestic sales of the same products. Or, export associations could be formed for this purpose.[2]

In addition to product standardization and pricing controls, MITI provided financial assistance. From 1953 through 1964, all or most export income was free of tax. Exporters were given deductions for the costs of establishing offices overseas. In 1964 this tax assistance was halted because it was found to violate GATT provisions against subsidizing exports. Certain other provisions have been used to promote exports, including increased depreciation for export sales, special tax treatment of reserves established for overseas market development, and tax exemption for income derived from exports of technology. Also, loans at reduced interest rates were provided to members of the cartel. The total value of interest-rate subsidy in 1980 was $566 million, according to U.S. Trade Representative William Brock.

The machine tool cartel also benefited from an unusual source of support. The government received more than $100 million in 1980 from bicycle and motorcycle racing. Under a 1948 law, this revenue was to be used to subsidize the bicycle industry, but MITI shifted to supporting the machine tool industry when alternative sources dried up. This race betting provides funds for research and technology to assist specific industries, including machine tools, through the Technical Research Institute of the Japan Society for the Promotion of Machine Industry. In 1981 the machine tool industry received six times the amount of support that the bicycle industry received from this fund.

As a result of documenting this assistance, the U.S. government concluded that an important export industry had been aggressively promoted. Specifically,

- Japan had protected its own domestic market against foreign competition, adopting countermeasures against liberalizing measures negotiated with its trading partners.
- Japan had supported and directed its machine tool industry through a series of extraordinary measures.
- Japan had funnelled billions of dollars of government funds to the industry.
- Japan's industry had engaged in collusive activity in concentrating production.
- Japan's penetration of the U.S. market had resulted in a demonstrable, unfavorable impact on the U.S. industry.

The Reagan administration examined the evidence and agreed with the principal facts presented. But the denial of tax credits was considered too draconian and potentially harmful to U.S. companies buying Japanese machine tools. Therefore, an alternative to the application of the tax laws also was considered. Under section 301 of the Trade Act of 1974, the president could have found that Japan had engaged in unfair trade practices, and he could have imposed quotas, tariffs, or other trade remedies.

The administration nevertheless concluded that neither law should apply. Too many other factors determined the success of Japanese machine tool exports. The fact that the Japanese prime minister made a special appeal to President Reagan for favorable consideration also may have helped. The result agreed upon by the United States and Japan was another compromise. They established a joint governmental "working group" to examine the problems of the industry and Japanese targeting methods — methods that have been known and used for almost sixty years.

CONCLUSION

For the purposes of describing trade management, two conclusions can be drawn. First, it is extremely difficult to deal with unfair trade practices, even when specific remedies are available under the trade or tax laws. Second, even though the demonstration of Japan's trade management through export assistance is overwhelming, neither the GATT nor U.S. law is adequate to the task of controlling the ways governments manage trade. There are too many uncertainties, too many constraints on government decisionmaking, and too many compromises available.

Later sections of this book will examine in more detail trade management in specific industries. The devices used to manage trade in textiles, steel, and automobiles involve more than the United States and Japan. Japan's policies for managing trade have been discussed for one simple reason: they are perceived to have been successful. As such they have provided a role model for advancing developing countries, for U.S. advocates of industrial policy, and for academic public administration experts everywhere. Japan's pattern of intervention in trade may well be the wave of the future.

NOTES

1. There is a significant body of opinion on the other side of this question, however, that denigrates MITI's role and influence. It cites the inherent characteristics of the Japanese people, their schooling and educational systems, the dynamism of the postwar business community, and the support of the United States as some of the other factors contributing to Japan's rapid rise. It is hard to argue with this view; at least one can say that MITI's influence has not hindered development. My own view is that it has significantly helped.
2. In 1982 U.S. law was changed to allow domestic competitors to form Export Trading Companies to agree on export arrangements previously illegal in the United States. In contrast to the Japanese provisions, domestic sales are still subject to antitrust.

6 REGIONAL TRADE BLOCS

The last chapter examined the effect of the policies of one country, Japan, on trade. Japan's conscious use of governmental tools to manage its trade have been successful in building one of the most dynamic and technologically advanced economies in the world. Its example has been and will be followed by a host of less developed imitators. In that sense Japan is itself a powerful force driving the world toward managed trade.

But Japan is clearly not alone and it is important to recognize many of the other forces at work. This chapter will concentrate on an equally, perhaps even more influential factor, that of countries banding together in trade blocs. In some cases, the association forms only for purposes of trade; in others, the association has broader aims. First to be analyzed is the "legality" of such associations under the GATT, followed by a description of the most prominent of these trade blocs and their impact as trade managers.

Some terminology will be useful at the outset. The GATT and economic theory distinguish between two kinds of trade blocs. A *free trade area* is a group of two or more countries that eliminate tariffs among themselves. In all other respects the members remain independent; they do not share a single customs service or a common tariff applied to other countries. The desired effect is to increase trade among the members of the free trade area.

A *customs union* is an association of two or more countries that not only eliminate tariffs between themselves but also erect common external tariffs against the rest of the world. They may or may not establish a single customs service, but even if the national services are retained, they apply a common tariff schedule. This may lead to other forms of integration, but those corollaries are not necessarily relevant to the trade bloc. The desired effects are both to increase trade among the members and to harmonize member treatment of nonmembers.

CUSTOMS UNIONS IN THE GATT

Various customs unions and free trade areas had existed for decades before the draftsmen of the GATT met in 1947 to establish the ground rules for postwar trade. The customs union of German states dating from 1834, and the even earlier union of the thirteen American colonies under the Articles of Confederation were only the most prominant examples. There was already in 1947 pressure in Europe to form a limited trade bloc among the six continental powers for coal, iron, and steel. The GATT drafters knew that some provisions must be included to cover the formation of such blocs.

The result incorporated in the General Agreement was an article dealing specifically with the conditions under which such trade blocs would be allowed. Article XXIV states in general that both free trade areas and customs unions can be allowed if they facilitate trade and do not raise barriers to nonmembers. More specifically, duties and other regulations of commerce "...shall not on the whole be higher or more restrictive than the general incidence..." before formation (see Dam 1970: 432). The meaning and interpretation of this provision have been disputed over the years, since there is no single way to measure "incidence" and the GATT contains no further guidance.

The absence of agreement on the precise application of these provisions has not prevented the GATT from considering and approving over a dozen trade bloc agreements. The most important was the 1956 Treaty of Rome establishing the six-member European Economic Community (EEC: originally France, Germany, Italy, Belgium, the Netherlands, and Luxembourg), but a number of others have been approved:

- the European Free Trade Association (the United Kingdom, Portugal, Switzerland, Scandinavia, and Ireland), 1961
- the Latin American Free Trade Area, 1961
- the Association of Greece with the EEC, 1963
- the Yaounde Convention (associating the former French colonies with the EEC), 1966
- the New Zealand/Australia Free-Trade Agreement, 1966
- the United Kingdom/Ireland Free-Trade Area Agreement, 1966

PROBLEMS OF TRADE BLOCS

It was assumed by the drafters of the GATT that free trade areas and customs unions were steps toward the ultimate goal of universal free trade. As one of the State Department negotiators put it in 1949, "A customs union creates a wider trading area, removes obstacles to competition, makes possible a more economic allocation of resources, and thus operates to increase production and raise planes of living. . . . A customs union is conducive to the expansion of trade on a basis of multilateralism and nondiscrimination. . ." (Wilcox 1949: 70–1; Dam 1970: 274–5).

These statements may be correct for the members of the union, but they are certainly not correct for others. A wider trading area is created for the members, but not necessarily for outsiders. Obstacles to competition are removed for members only; new ones can be created for nonmembers. The system is "multilateral" only for the participants. And finally, it is inherently discriminatory. It can be argued that any and every such agreement violates not only the spirit but also the letter of the most sacred and fundamental GATT principle: that all GATT member states are to be treated equally.

It must be assumed that the GATT drafters knew something of these practical implications of allowing trade blocs. They may not have fully understood all of the economic ramifications so clearly discussed by Dam and other observers, but the discriminatory element does not require extensive economic analysis to see.

On the contrary, later commentators seem to believe that the discrimination was the price that had to be paid for reviving Europe. Patterson's conclusion is that in a conflict between the GATT and the drive to build the European Common Market, the GATT would have lost and been destroyed.[1] Thus the basic principle of national treatment, requiring all GATT members to be treated equally, was quietly abandoned in favor of more powerful forces of trade management.

But even that result would not necessarily be adverse for world trade if, in fact, trade blocs lead to a more efficient international economy, as the drafters had supposed. If trade blocs enhance the market forces allocating capital and resources, then their conflict with basic principles might be acceptable after all. The problem is that the "trade creation" effects of such blocs cannot be demonstrated nearly as well as the "trade diversion" effects. In other words, economists can show clearly that nonmember trade is diverted from the bloc; but they only speculate that more trade is created because of increased activity within the bloc itself.

Take for example a U.S. exporter of a product such as a basic chemical in which quality and brand can be eliminated as factors influencing the buyer's choice. Assume the exporter had 50 percent of the French market before France became a member of the European Economic Community, with the rest supplied by Germany. Both the United States and Germany would face the same French tariff levels. Upon formation of the Common Market, France would have to lower the tariff applicable to German imports to zero, but it would maintain a common tariff against the United States at some level (averaged among the six countries forming the Common Market). The rational French buyer would shift all of his purchases to the lower cost German supplies, and the U.S. exporter would have to divert his exports to other markets, perhaps lowering his prices to gain market share.

Thus there are several expected results of the formation of such a trade bloc:

- Trade will increase among the members.
- Members will have lower costs of production, based on the absence of tariffs on some raw materials and intermediate products.
- Based on lower costs, members will be more competitive internationally.
- Trade from nonmembers will be adversely affected.
- Investment within the bloc will increase as former exporters become investors to get under the common external tariff.
- Trade from former exporters will be diverted from the bloc to other destinations.

- As a result of trade diversion, prices for some diverted commodities will fall because of excess supply, or else production outside the bloc will be cut back.

Thus the impact of a trade bloc is protectionist, achieving all of the goals of quotas and high tariffs, yet doing so with the GATT's blessing. As Dam concludes, "...it becomes clear that customs unions or free-trade areas complying fully with the requirements of paragraphs 5 through 8 of Article XXIV may be strongly protectionist in effect" (see Dam 1970: 283).

THE EUROPEAN ECONOMIC COMMUNITY

Let us turn from this theoretical discussion of what could happen to what actually has happened. We will first review some of the effects on trade of the creation of the European Common Market, and then take a briefer look at some of the other trade blocs that today manage significant shares of world trade. A later chapter will examine the special problems of the East bloc and East–West trade.

The driving force in the creation of the Common Market was a Frenchman, Jean Monnet, an experienced international businessman and financier. From his post at the French Planning Office, under de Gaulle, he began the task of rebuilding France. His objective was to plan by bringing ideas and people together rather than by issuing directives. He sought to combine planning with the market system, first in France and then later in Western Europe as a whole. The term adopted for this system is "indicative planning," which only worked through persuasion and consent (Johnson 1983: 590–1).

After the war he began to encourage the Western European leaders to follow the example of Belgium and Luxembourg, which had already in 1921 formed a common customs union.[2] After the war they were joined by the Netherlands, setting up a common external tariff in 1948. This led to the establishment in 1951 of the European Coal and Steel Community, with the three joined by France, Germany and Italy. Recovery in Europe required rebuilding, as quickly as possible, the basic steel industry upon which so many other industries depend. In order to plan the rebuilding and minimize competition between national industries, the Coal and Steel Community set out to combine a common market for coal and steel with a managed industry. A common external tariff for these products was established, the fore-runner of the full Common Market.

Six years later in 1957, the six countries agreed to establish the general Common Market covering all products, to end all restrictions on the movement of persons, goods and capital, and to begin the process of harmonizing laws and regulatory systems. The Treaty of Rome, which established the European Economic Community, set up the processes and the substantive rules that have guided the EEC to this day.

The very structure of the EEC and its associated states is discriminatory. First, nonmembers are of course treated differently from members, in violation of the most-favored nation principles of the GATT. Furthermore, certain associated states are given preferences over other states that are not associated, thus compounding the problem. Sugar exporters in African countries that were formerly colonies of France, for example, were part of the Yaounde and later Lome Convention groups that were granted lower tariffs than other sugar producers. As a result, they may have better market access than sugar producers elsewhere. While the United States may be able to turn the other cheek because of its economic strength and its role in supporting the creation of the EEC, other countries may not feel quite so magnanimous. The burden has fallen with particular force on Latin American and Asian countries never colonized by the European powers.

The EEC has also discriminated against certain countries, such as Japan and the East bloc, in order to preserve its freedom of action against imports from those areas. These countries compete with a broad range of EEC industries, and therefore have been denied the full protection of the GATT's provisions, even though Japan, Hungary, Poland, and Romania are members. There have also been more technical deviations from specialized GATT agreements denying their protection to other countries in particular cases. The result is clear: the EEC has institutionalized and legitimized trade discrimination in a massive way.

There is no doubt that the EEC has contributed to the growth and expansion of the Western European economies. Great strides have been made, by opening up internal markets, providing more equitable and efficient investment decisionmaking, and allowing freedom of movement. The members of the Community have benefited, and the original six were joined by three full members in 1973, the United Kingdom, Ireland, and Denmark; by an associated member, Greece, which later became a full member; by associated countries such as Israel, Cyprus and Turkey; by two other countries negotiating membership, Spain and Portugal; and by a large number of former colonies in Africa and the Caribbean. The success is evident for all to see and for some to share.

THE COSTS OF THE EEC

Economic success has come at a price, however. Part of that price has been paid by countries denied opportunities to trade in Europe — opportunities that would have been available in the absence of the discriminatory treatment of nonmembers. Another price has been paid by the international system by having its most fundamental principle, most-favored nation treatment, cavalierly set aside. And the most lasting effect of the Common Market may be its legitimizing the bilateral and sectoral "deals" that have become so prominent a part of EEC trade policy.

The internal workings of the Community's decisionmaking will not be discussed in detail here. There are, however, several points to be made. Since the EEC Council has used a rule of unanimity in voting on important questions, any country may in effect veto an action in the best interests of the others. In the trade area this means that the most protectionist views must be given heed, and frequently they set the tone for the Community as a whole. Another aspect of Community operation is that, as a customs union, it must speak with one voice in trade negotiations. If one country takes a position protecting its steel industry, that will also be the Community position, regardless of the views of more liberal governments.

In recent years the limits of the Council's secretariat and courts have become clear. And wherever national interests have not been "Europeanized", there remains a great deal of independent action. Even in the supposedly harmonized trade area, for instance, the members have markedly different policies toward imports of Japanese automobiles. These range from an essentially totally open market in Belgium, a country without any national automakers, to essentially closed markets in Italy and France, countries with nationalized automakers. The members also have different policies and linkages with the Eastern European countries, stemming in part from historical ties. In spite of these differences, however, the Community has had a major impact on the shape of world trade since 1957.

THE EEC'S SECTORAL POLICIES

The EEC has adopted a number of explicit "industrial policies" to modify free market behavior, starting with the iron and steel policies and the agricultural support programs. The impact of these has not been favorable when viewed against the aspirations and commitments of the GATT. Nowhere is this more evident than in agriculture, the area of greatest central control and support. The Rome Treaty itself called for the six original members to establish a Common Agricultural Policy, the infamous CAP. Exporters of farm products to Europe feared that the EEC would use the CAP to erect barriers to imports in order to encourage self-sufficiency and to build incomes for farmers, always a potent political group in every country.

When the policy was announced in 1962, the CAP provided, in the words of one seasoned observer ". . . about as potentially a watertight system of protection as the human mind could devise" (Patterson 1983: 228). The system included "indicative" prices, variable levies to reach these prices, restitution payments and export subsidies. In grains, sugar, dairy products, and beef, the EEC has not only reversed its traditional dependence on imports (still the case as recently as 1974) but has become a net exporter. In 1981 half of EEC farm spending, already the largest item in the EEC budget, went for export subsidies.

It has been the U.S. view that the EEC's policies are very disruptive to an efficient world trading system in agriculture. In several of the semi-annual EEC–U.S. trade policy discussions, the CAP was defended vigorously by the EEC leaders. Paradoxically, they also discussed the changes being considered to lessen its costs, and thus its adverse impact. The expected reforms have not yet materialized. On the one hand, the EEC cites its crushing fiscal burden; on the other hand, the export subsidies to eliminate its mounting farm surpluses continue to rise. In the absence of major reforms of the Community's political processes, which give such overwhelming weight to agricultural protectionism, the Community necessarily will continue to manage its agricultural sector through export subsidies.

A later chapter will examine two sectors in which the EEC's influence has been similarly malignant, steel and textiles. In both areas the EEC has pushed relentlessly for increased "management" of the trade in these products. The results reflect the EEC's penchant for negotiating deals between countries to solve trade problems. These negotiations take the place of the operation of the market or the more neutral rules of the game. As such, both bilateralism and sectoral policy threaten the entire world economy. The threat was stated clearly by the director general of the GATT, Arthur Dunkel, in 1982:

> The tendency toward bilateralism and sectoralism in trade policy is the greatest present danger both politically and economically to order and prosperity in the world economy. In political terms it must undermine the credibility of those in industrialized countries who champion the open trading system and commend it to the developing world. More profoundly, it endangers the very possibility of maintaining the international economic cooperation which has made possible the progress of the last 30 years: for that cooperation can only be based on multilateralism and obedience to general rules (Dunkel 1982).

THE BILATERALISM OF TRADE BLOCS

There are several problems with bilateral deals in trade. First, those who are not party to the agreement may suspect that the burden of the solution to the trade problem will fall on them. Second, bilateral agreements are not always made public so that the terms can be considered. Third, agreements reached outside of the GATT (as so many are) are not necessarily reviewed by third parties to ensure their conformity to the GATT's often detailed rules. For all of these reasons bilateral deals undermine the system.

Bilateral deals hurt in other ways. Most often they are concerned with a particular problem in a particular sector, such as autos or steel. The solution frequently reached in such bilateral negotiations is not surprising. It normally takes a protectionist turn, and leads to restraints on trade of one kind or another to "solve" the problem. An orderly marketing arrangement, a voluntary export restraint, or some other device is agreed upon to relieve the import pressure. Since government has now temporarily abrogated the harsh realities of the market, trade is successfully managed in the short run.

But the short run often turns into the long run. The bilateral agreement creates vested interest in both seller and buyer. An impacted domestic industry, complaining about imports, prolongs the protection. Even the exporting industry may agree that part of the market is better than none and may support the restraint. Thus, once imposed, they are hard to dislodge.

Bilateral sectoral deals rigidify the trading system. They are the essence of the attempt to manage trade between two countries. The point is not that there would be no bilateralism without the EEC, but rather that the structure of the EEC, and the domestic pressures created and focused by it, have given much greater impetus to the trend. Bilateral deals remove firms, industries, and whole sectors from the multilateral system of agreed rules. They diminish, perhaps even disable, the market forces that the open trading system is expected to preserve. And they give increased power to the large blocs and trading countries that can use their markets to force deals from smaller or weaker trading partners.

OTHER TRADE BLOCS

The West Europeans are not alone in attempting through trade blocs to increase their bargaining position in managing their trade. Europe had produced another group, the European Free Trade Area (EFTA), composed of those trading countries left out of the original Common Market. While agreeing to eliminate tariffs and trade barriers among themselves, the EFTA countries never established a common external tariff against other countries, and thus never reached the stage of a customs union. EFTA was in some respects a counterweight to the EEC, but weakened when major EFTA countries joined the EEC.

The Latin American countries have tried numerous experiments to remove barriers between themselves, and almost all have failed. The Latin American Free Trade Area, the Central American Common Market, the Andean Common Market, and even the Caribbean Common Market have all been established with great hopes and fanfare, only to disappear as in effective arrangements. The basic problem is political, since the differences between forms of government are greater than the similarities of economies or the benefits of free trade among them. Latin countries have traditionally looked north to the United States and across the Atlantic to Europe, rather than across mountains or rivers to each other. Even more limited groupings, such as the Andean Pact countries, fail because of their political differences.

Nevertheless, the purpose of such unions is clear. Governments are attempting to control and influence trade and investment by intervening in the market. Countries offer incentives to new investment, subsidies to exports, controls on imports, nontariff barriers to imports, and incentives to trade between bloc members. But they also pursue nationalist economic policies to protect local industry. Foreign traders and investors must deal with exporting requirements, local-content requirements, technology transfer requirements, and earnings repatriation requirements limiting their freedom of action. These trade-managing policies protect domestic infant industries, but frequently more political goals are also being pursued. The intervention of the government in trade provides the tools; the politicians and local business community provide the goals.

Africa has similarly experimented with a variety of arrangements to manage trade. Both East Africa and West Africa have established separate customs areas, but since there is so little trade between African economies, they have had little impact. The more important relationships for almost all African states revert to the European colonial powers. Thus the original agreement between the former French colonies and the EEC, the Yaounde Agreement, provided for lower tariffs (preferences) for these countries. Their products were given preferred treatment and better market opportunities than those of other developing countries. Later, the arrangement was extended in time and broadened in area to include the former colonies of the United Kingdom.

The potentially most potent of these trade blocs to be set up in emulation of the EEC is the Association of South East Asian Nations (ASEAN). This group of five countries, all with similar political interests, and with dynamic and growing economies, may be on the road to establishing a market similar to the EEC. The countries — Thailand, Malaysia, Singapore, Indonesia, and the Philippines — share anticommunist ideals and capitalist economies. They have begun to act in coordination in their dealings with the United States and the EEC, edging toward one voice in trade matters. Among themselves they are coordinating development plans and allocating new projects. Although they have not yet established a common market or a customs union, trade among them is increasingly free. Given their present strength, skilled workforce, large populations, and rich resources, they have great potential.

As their relative share of world production continues to grow, so too will their voice in trade matters. When the ASEAN group begins to flex its muscles, another powerful participant will join the United States, Japan, and the EEC in the formation of world trade policies. Its perspective will differ, but its interest is great in preserving the open world trading system. At the GATT ministerial meeting in November 1982, there were several occasions on which the ASEAN group opposed initiatives that it considered potentially restrictive of trade. It is likely that ASEAN will play an increasingly important role in support of the GATT system.

THE U.S. RESPONSE

The last developments in the creation of trade blocs are the efforts of the United States itself. The earlier review of limited trade arrangements touched on the U.S. Canadian Auto Pact. The two countries agreed in 1963 to allow essentially free trade in autos and automotive parts between themselves. It is generally believed that this pact has allowed the development of an automobile industry in Canada, even though ownership of it has remained largely in U.S. hands. The two countries are now exploring, at Canada's initiative, similar arrangements for other industries, such as agricultural equipment, chemicals, steel, and computers.

More ambitious plans for a North American Common Market, including Mexico, have been politically shelved. In 1979 Congress mandated a study of the potential for such an arrangement. The study, produced by the Commerce Department and the U.S. trade agencies, showed that benefits would flow to all three participating countries, but that the practical problems of connecting the smaller Canadian economy and less developed Mexican economy to the behemoth between them were insurmountable. As might be expected, the report sank without a splash.

Even if the plans for the North American Common Market are premature, the United States has taken some other steps that may show a more promising path. At President Reagan's urging, Congress passed the Caribbean Basin Initiative (CBI), which grants for twelve years, duty-free entry for products made in the Caribbean Islands and Central America. Access to the U.S. market was recognized as a powerful development incentive, which led to the proposal. It is not clear whether the initiative would have been proposed without the regional challenge of Cuba and its ally Nicaragua. Discussions of the proposal within the administration made it clear that the initiative's political and defense motivations were as important as the developmental ones.

The House Ways and Means Committee, however, had questions that revolved around the impact of duty-free admission of Caribbean imports on U.S. domestic industries. As a result of those concerns and heavy lobbying by the industries most likely to be affected, several important exceptions were included to prevent apparel, leather goods, and footwear from receiving duty-free entry. These are, of course, some of the sectors that are often successful in the less developed islands and whose volume of output would be unlikely to harm U.S. manufacturers. Nevertheless, the special treatment was denied. Many other opportunities remain, however, and the long-run effect of the CBI on the region will be positive.

The important point to make in conclusion is that the United States is now itself part of trade blocs. Granted, the step was a limited one that did not demand reciprocal free access to the Caribbean countries; the trade area operates only one way, into the United States. A more equitable bloc has been negotiated with Israel for free trade in both directions between Israel and the United States. Other countries may also see advantages in concluding free trade arrangements with the United States.

This movement presents a challenge to the GATT system, but it is a movement that should be endorsed. As long as the advantages to the participants of preferential arrangements outweigh the disadvantages, they will be negotiated. The EEC has led the way, and other regions around the world have followed while the United States looked the other way. As long as the United States proceeds prudently and limits its arrangements to special cases where it has demonstrable interests, such as the Caribbean and Israel, there can be little objection from those who have pursued similar arrangements with much more restrictive effect. That is another way trade will be managed, through the increasing number and power of trade blocs, and the United States will be a part of the movement.

NOTES

1. See, for example, the comment by Patterson quoted in Dam (1970: 263).
2. It is worth pointing out that all of the customs unions formed before World War II were between very small ministates and the neighboring "protector": Monaco and France, San Marino and Italy, Liechtenstein and Switzerland, and Luxembourg and Belgium. Obviously the effects of such customs unions were quite limited and in no way justified the much larger postwar unions.

7 TRADE FINANCE AND SUBSIDIES

There are two different types of subsidy problems. The first relates primarily to country efforts to promote exports. Many countries employ subsidies of many different kinds to stimulate exports and help their producers find and develop foreign markets. These subsidies may take the form of outright grants, tax refunds or rebates, lower cost loans, reduced prices on raw materials, duty-free imports, government ownership, accelerated depreciation, training grants, overseas marketing support, and below-market trade financing, among many others.

The second problem occurs between developed countries, although others may soon begin to feel the same pressures. It revolves around the regulation and monitoring of export assistance given through long-term loans. The United States uses the Export-Import Bank (Ex-Im) and several other government programs for this purpose, and most other developed countries have similar institutions. The United Kingdom uses an agency within its Department of Trade; West Germany and France use independent agencies.

Regardless of form, in every case the rationale is the same. Exports of substantial magnitude, such as aircraft, nuclear power plants, and major construction projects and equipment, require long-term financing, especially when the buyer is a developing country. Governments can provide these loans at lower interest rates and with longer repayment schedules than private sources can. Furthermore, there is an element of aid to the economic development of the borrower in lending which would not be forthcoming from private sources.

Another type of subsidy for exports is provided by international lending banks like the World Bank, the Inter-American Development Bank, and its counterparts for Asia and Africa. Although the primary purpose of their loans and grants is the development of roads, dams, and other infrastructure, they also make loans to national development banks. These banks lend directly to industry. Often the projects financed or supported by the institutions are geared to supplying export markets. At a minimum, they affect trade by subsidizing firms making products to supply the local market and thus replace imports.

SUBSIDIES AND THE GATT

The treatment of subsidies in the GATT has been influenced to a large degree by U.S. views and pressures. U.S. legislation has allowed the imposition of countervailing duties to offset the impermissible subsidies of other governments. This practice dates from 1890 when a statute was passed allowing the imposition of duties to offset the bounties paid by other governments promoting the export of sugar. In 1897 the statute was broadened to cover all imports, and it has been on the books ever since. Other countries (France, Japan, Spain, Switzerland, and others) enacted similar laws before World War II. In addition, about thirty bilateral treaties outlawing bounties or subsidies were negotiated in the heyday of free trade between 1860 and 1920.

Thus by the time the General Agreement was drafted in 1947, the idea was well established that certain kinds of subsidies were inconsistent with free trade. Article VI of the GATT was included to sanction the imposition of countervailing duties by member governments to offset "any bounty or subsidy bestowed directly or indirectly, upon the manufacture, production, or export of any merchandise," language paralleling U.S. law.

However, the definition of what kinds of subsidies were permissible and what kinds were countervailable was not satisfactorily drafted then, or in the intervening thirty-five years. Out of this confusion have arisen decades of disputes between countries. In 1955 the developed GATT members agreed to limit export subsidies to certain primary products. But this limitation did not cover developing countries.

Moreover, the definition of the export subsidies hinged upon a test similar to dumping products; that is, the exports were priced lower than the same goods on the domestic market. This test proved to be unworkable. In 1960 the GATT formed a committee to examine the question. It resulted in a list of practices defined as export subsidies, following U.S. court and administrative decisions on countervailing duties (Hufbauer 1983: 343).

During the Tokyo Round of negotiations, a code to further define regulated subsidies and the actions that may be taken against them was drafted and adopted by the United States and other major trading nations. This code was necessary because the existing GATT provisions did not adequately define subsidies. The code also clarifies the self-help countries may use in combating subsidies. Countries may impose countervailing duties when their domestic industries suffer "material injury" through falling sales or employment, rising shares of imports, or falling prices due to imports. In the absence of material injury, a country may still complain to the GATT of a clearly evident export subsidy. If the complaint is accepted, then the complaining country may impose a countervailing duty or withdraw a previous trade concession to the subsidizing country.

This code contains an illustrative list of prohibited subsidies, based on the earlier 1960 effort. Although it attempts to clarify the definitions, in many ways it further complicates the issues. For example, the list states that if a country provides goods to its manufacturers on terms less favorable than the world market price, but still subsidized, then exports manufactured with those goods are not counteravailable. In other words, the existence of a subsidy is not enough; its effect in terms of market prices must also be examined. Similarly, if a country provides export credits at rates below the cost of money to the government, that would appear to be a subsidy. The GATT code defines it as a subsidy only if the rate is below that agreed in the Organization for Economic Cooperation and Development (OECD) arrangement on export credits.

The most technical and perennial dispute concerning export subsidies involves taxes. The GATT itself allows the rebate of indirect taxes; but the rebate of direct taxes is a subsidy. European and other value-added tax systems tax products at each stage of production, payable by the seller. These systems also exempt exports from taxation, since the purchaser is outside the country of origin. This approach is accepted by the Subsidies Code. The problem lies in the fact that the European value-added taxes, like U.S. income taxes, are the primary revenue sources; but unlike the value-added taxes, U.S. income taxes apply to all income, from foreign sales as well as domestic.

In order to partially equalize the tax burdens, the United States adopted in 1971 a provision of U.S. tax law allowing the establishment of Domestic International Sales Corporations (DISCs). In essence, the tax on part of a DISC's income that derived from exports was deferred until the income was brought home. The Europeans thought this device too transparent a dodge around the GATT provisions, and they complained. A GATT panel, convened to judge the case, decided that unless interest was charged on the deferred taxes, it constituted an illegal export subsidy. After years of wrangling, the United States finally agreed and pledged to change its DISC legislation.

The changes were enacted into law in July 1984. DISCs may continue for small exporters, and for those who pay interest as the GATT requires. But for the majority of large exporters, a new device called the Foreign Sales Corporation (FSC) is authorized. The primary difference is that the new FSC must be set up overseas, whereas the earlier DISC could be a "paper" U.S. corporation. The new FSC is thus treated like any other foreign subsidiary, and the income of the FSC is not taxed in the United States until repatriated.

To some degree this legislation restores the level playing field so eagerly sought by U.S. policymakers. U.S. exports, through FSCs, are subject to the same type of territorial tax system that the Europeans used during the 1960s and 1970s. The added administrative costs and inconveniences of meeting the requirements of the FSC legislation will be minimized through the creation of new services in foreign jurisdictions designed to handle FSC transactions. Already, major manufacturers are actively exploring their options, and lawyers and accountants are rushing to fill the need.

A question about the compatibility of the FSC with the GATT may remain, however. The Europeans still have the option of complaining that the FSC itself meets the definition of an export subsidy. As long as the Europeans and the other countries can keep the United States on the defensive about its own DISC and FSC laws, U.S. zeal in pursuing its subsidies must be tempered. Thus the question of what constitutes a countervailable export subsidy will remain a subject of debate for some time to come.

DOMESTIC SUBSIDIES

The GATT and the Subsidies Code have recognized for some time that the problems of government subsidization interfering with trade is much broader than the pure case of export subsidies. There is a wide range of government activities involving the domestic economy that can and will have an effect on exports and imports. Just how far into the domestic economy should a subsidy complaint reach? Which practices are justified and which are outside the common understanding? These are the questions now coming to the fore.

The most extreme position is that any subsidy, regardless of type or purpose, interferes with the free market and is therefore objectionable. Even purely domestic subsidies will have an international impact. They will make domestic products cheaper to domestic consumers, compensate for the higher costs of raw materials or skilled labor, and generally favor a domestic industry over a foreign one. Imports will suffer even if exports are not subsidized. Therefore any support should be countervailable, in the interests of spreading the free market as far as possible and protecting the unsubsidized domestic industry from unfairly supported foreign competition. This has traditionally been the U.S. position, dating back to at least 1903, and limited only by the practicalities of gaining international acceptance of it (Hufbauer 1983: 351).

This extreme view has normally been supported by the U.S. Congress in its attempts to write the countervailing duty laws as broadly as possible. The U.S. Treasury Department, however, before 1973 clung to a more limited view focused solely on export subsidies. It denied petitions for countervailing duties unless the intent of the foreign government was clearly to support exports. A major decision in 1973 levied countervailing duties against tires imported from Canada by the Michelin Company. In that case, the assistance given by the Canadian province to attract the tire plant was considered counteravailable. This decision began the process of broadening U.S. law. Later, in a 1975 case against float glass the Treasury stated a "rule of reason" in such cases. Regional subsidies had to create a trade distortion to be attackable; if they were small or aided firms with few exports, or were merely offsetting higher local costs, they were acceptable.

Congress disapproved of this approach by passing the Trade Act of 1979. This act brought into U.S. law the provisions of the Subsidies

Code, including the notion that subsidies "granted with the aim of giving an advantage to certain industries" were countervailable. This means that general assistance through labor training programs, uniform tax credits, or general help for railroads are all permissible, but industry-specific assistance is not. Further support for this view was given in a U.S. court decision in 1980 that struck down the "rule of reason" used by the Treasury under the pre-1979 law. The failure of the Treasury Department to interpret broadly the congressional mandate was one reason the authority for deciding countervailing duty cases was shifted from the Treasury to the Commerce Department in 1980.

Subsequent decisions have confirmed that the United States considers a broad range of domestic subsidies as countervailable. In 1982, for instance, the United States imposed duties to offset a Mexican regional subsidy program that assisted its ceramic tile industry (Federal Register 1982). In another decision the Commerce Department found (and the International Trade Court confirmed) that equity investments made by the British government in British Steel Corporation, in circumstances in which a "prudent investor" would not invest, also constitutes a countervailable subsidy.

An even more important emerging area is the problem of upstream subsidies—those subsidies on inputs to exports. In another 1982 decision, the Commerce Department treated European upstream subsidies to the coking coal industry as not objectionable under complaints about steel imports. The test was the final price of the coal. As long as the subsidies did not bring the price below world prices, there was no countervailable subsidy. In other cases, however, where the input is subsidized below world price, the duties could be imposed on products made from those subsidized inputs.

Two other emerging subsidy problems have been identified. These involve first, the growing arena of state-owned, or partly state-owned and financed industries; and second, state-supported research and development programs. In both areas the intent of government is to preserve an industrial base and to improve international competitiveness. In the case of loans made to exporters, or investments made in them, the U.S. practice now is to look at the distortions caused by covering operating losses, cross-subsidization of products, and targeting of export markets. Loans at market rates or equity purchases on the open market do not entail subsidy, regardless of the purpose for which they are made. Therefore the United States must examine both the creditworthiness of the supported firm and the domestic market for its shares before looking at the distortions caused.

The problems of government research and development programs have yet to receive full treatment. Although support for basic research is a legitimate government function according to the U.S. view, applied product development assistance is out of bounds. The problems of defining basic and applied research are compounded by the practice of governments targeting their funding (whether for basic or applied) on certain industries with export potential. If the results of the research are not made available to the community as a whole, but are used to promote the interests of particular firms or research consortia, then the subsidy is palpable.

EXPORT CREDITS AND THE OECD

Consider now the related issue of subsidies by developed countries to promote exports through export credits. There is no question of definition here, since the export credits are so named by most countries using them. All of the industrialized countries use some form of official credit facility or program to finance exports. The amounts of money involved are huge; in 1979, for example, Japan's authorization was almost $40 billion, followed by the United Kingdom with $33 billion, France with $32 billion, and Germany with $14.5 billion. The United Kingdom had the highest proportion among the seven major industrialized nations with almost 48 percent of manufactured exports covered by export credits, followed by France (42.5 percent), Japan (39.7 percent) and Italy (13.1 percent) (Hufbauer 1983: 331).

The U.S. credit program for 1979 was $9.5 billion, or 8 percent of the value of manufactured U.S. exports. It is largely under the Export-Import Bank, but there are commodity credit programs at the Department of Agriculture, and a few other small export credit programs are available. It is interesting to note in passing that the U.S. Export-Import Bank was established in 1934 with the purpose of financing exports to the Soviet Union, a purpose which it did not fulfill then and under current policies cannot fulfill today.

The United States has always been ambivalent about export credits. The exporting industries are ardent supporters and lobby strenuously for export credit expansion. They point out the extensive programs abroad and the need to remain competitive not only in product but also in financing. Economists generally oppose export credits as an inefficient subsidy that draws resources from other industries, favors exporters, generally favors buyers over sellers, and incurs a significant budgetary cost.

Government officials are caught in the middle, supporting credits as a necessary evil until they can be eliminated or at least better regulated. As Hufbauer concludes from his examination, "[they] clearly illustrate why the United States feels aggrieved: its subsidy programs are consistently smaller, and in some instances trending downwards, by comparison with its major competitors" (Hufbauer 1983: 333). The uneven playing field that existed throughout the 1970s ensured that the subsidy issue would remain in the foreground.

Efforts have been successful in the last few years to level the playing field. The industrialized countries of the OECD have reached agreement on disciplines intended to eliminate, as far as possible, competition between national treasuries in exporting. While these arrangements are not perfect, they have substantially tightened the controls over export credits. As a result the competition for export sales is gradually returning to commercial considerations rather than focusing on national credits. The process is not yet complete, but progress is being made.

The chairman of the OECD's Export Credit Group is Axel Wallen of Sweden, an experienced and knowledgeable international diplomat. In his address to the U.S. Export-Import Bank, during its fiftieth anniversary celebration, Dr. Wallen explained the history of the export credit problem.

Export credits first became widespread after the First World War, when so many countries realized they needed to subsidize growth. The first form of support was in export insurance, designed to reduce the risk of selling to foreign buyers. Without the insurance, a seller could not risk the default of the buyer or the failure to be paid in a usable currency.

After World War II, the greatest uses of export credits were found in shipbuilding. There was excess capacity in shipbuilding; Japan and Europe were rebuilding their trade and expanding their economies. The result was a bidding war between countries to support, through subsidies, the export of ships to keep the shipyards busy. At the end of the 1960s, the major shipbuilding countries, except for the United States, reached agreement in the OECD to end the bidding war and to limit the amounts and types of subsidies provided in this sector.

While this agreement was being discussed, another OECD group concerned with export credits broached a more general agreement covering all exports, not just ships. Their discussions were given great impetus after the 1973 oil crisis when it became apparent that there would be increased competition among the developed industrialized countries to pay their higher oil bills to OPEC. This was also the period of rapidly rising competition from the newly industrializing countries in supplying the needs of the developing countries and the East Europeans.

After several years of negotiations, six countries provided "unilateral" declarations (a sort of gentleman's agreement) not to go below certain levels in their export credits. The agreement actually set a floor under interest rates, stating that no one would charge less or give better terms. It distinguished between the very poor countries, given the lowest interest rates (7 percent) and the longest repayment terms (ten years), and the relatively well-off developing countries, given the highest rates (8.5 percent) and shortest repayment period (five years), with intermediate countries to be offered rates and terms in between.

This matrix of rates and terms depending on development status still survives, although the rates and terms have been modified many times since 1976, to take account of market rates. In 1978 the agreement was formalized by all OECD members. In the early 1980s, when market rates were substantially above the agreement levels, the members decided to adjust the interest rates. Special arrangements were developed for aircraft and nuclear power plant sales; and for including advanced developing countries, such as the East bloc, in the group charged the highest rates. Most recently, attempts are being made to limit the amount of subsidy in total to an agreed level of approximately 50 percent. This will effectively regulate the new practice of mixing export credit and outright assistance (such as U.S. AID funds) in order to make a sale.

The characteristics of the arrangement may be described briefly. First, the OECD countries agree not to subsidize exports to each others' countries through government export credits. This means that the U.S. Export-Import Bank, for example, will not finance or guarantee loans for exports to France, Japan, or any other OECD member. The Ex-Im Bank's programs are therefore available to the rest of the world, as are the official credit programs of the other OECD nations. Second, the OECD countries have agreed on the terms and conditions of official export credits, standardizing them to a certain extent. They also have agreed on a schedule of interest rates, and other provisions for credits. In theory all OECD countries abide by these provisions.

Achieving this degree of harmony was not easy since the very essence of these programs is to support national exports in competition with other countries. As countries in the early 1980s began to see the enormous cost of these programs, they sought to limit their budgetary impact. At the same time, however, the countries realized that a major subsidized export sale may in fact be cheaper than having plants close and workers on the dole. This was particularly true in the Western European states with costly welfare programs. The problem of export credit subsidies has been ameliorated but not eliminated.

CURRENT ISSUES

A major problem facing the developed industrial countries has been the treatment of credits from Japan and a few other low-interst rate countries. The cost of money to the Japanese government is the rate at which its citizens buy government bonds or continue to save in its Postal Savings System — the largest source of government debt finance. In 1982 the Japanese government cost of money was around 5 to 6 percent. For the United States and most of Western Europe, the costs of money were considerably higher, ranging from 12 to 18 percent. The OECD countries agreed on the 12 percent figure (as they did for the middle-income borrowers), after considerable negotiation. This meant that although subsidies were limited for some countries, there was actually a "negative subsidy", or premium, placed on Japanese credits. The official Japanese credits had higher interest rates than the cost of money to the government.

The "mixed credit" problem has also arisen. Suppose, for example, that a country granted not only an official export credit under the terms of the OECD agreement, but also a direct grant or very low-interest (say 1 or 2 percent) loan under an aid program. Suppose also that the aid was given with the stipulation that it could only be used to purchase goods from the donor country, a not unusual condition. The combination of official export credit plus aid would be lower than the official credit alone. In this way the exporting country would both abide by the OECD arrangement and give the importing country better terms.

France has been the largest practitioner and exponent of mixed credits. Other countries, led by the United States, have opposed the practice as subverting the intent and the letter of the OECD arrangement. U.S. attempts over the last few years to have mixed credits limited have failed. As a result, there is now support in the United States and in the Congress for fighting fire with fire, using mixed credits to match similar credits offered by other countries. The practice should not be a permanent part of U.S. policy, however, because it allows too much competition between governments outside the OECD agreement.

Another problem, which emerged in the early 1980s, was the credit terms available to the East bloc. A number of Western European countries and Japan have substantial trade with the Soviet Union and the other East European countries. A significant proportion of this trade has been subsidized through export credits granted by both Western governments and Western banks. Under the OECD arrangement, the East bloc borrowers were given terms as favorable as the lowest income countries, even though their per capita incomes were considerably higher. Furthermore, it made little sense to tighten the controls on the flow of technology and productive equipment for defense industries, and for the oil and gas industries, while simultaneously granting generous subsidies to the same countries. As a result of U.S. pressure, the OECD countries agreed in 1982 to raise the interest rates for the Eastern borrowers to the level of the highest income borrowers. While the rates are still below market, the amount of subsidy has been significantly reduced.

Finally, the OECD countries have addressed the particular problems of financing commercial aircraft and nuclear power plants. Official export credits have played a major role in these two industries. In fact, one of the frequent complaints heard about the Ex-Im Bank is that it is really Boeing's bank. About two-thirds of all Ex-Im lending goes to these two industries, so the claim is not farfetched; the competition between the U.S. producers and government-supported consortia has been intense.

The European Airbus is significantly subsidized by its sponsoring governments and has penetrated a number of markets previously held by Boeing and McDonnell Douglas. Some of this penetration has been achieved through low-cost export credits, although political and diplomatic strings have also been pulled, in violation of the 1979 GATT Aircraft Code.[1] The technical and commercial features of the Airbus have been assisted and sometimes overshadowed by this government support. The story is much the same in the nuclear power plant industry, where each sale involves so many billions of dollars and is so important for the long-term health of the exporting industry that all stops are pulled in making the sale.

An attempt has been made to reduce the competition between treasuries in the sale of both aircraft and nuclear power industries by agreeing on specific interest rates and repayment schedules offered to borrowers. In general these provisions have been accepted, but every time a sale is lost the allegations start flying again that the winner violated these understandings. Fortunately the sales are so big and so carefully scrutinized by all of the bidders that any irregularities become evident.

It is necessary to be on the lookout for violations and to continue to seek ways to tighten the disciplines in these two areas in which temptation is so great. Without this attentiveness, the countries with the deepest pockets and the greatest willingness to subsidize will distort the efficiencies of the market. And that is the fundamental problem of subsidies, no matter how attractive they may appear to consumers and importers.

In the long run, export subsidies preserve industries that are no longer viable; turn companies into mendicants for export help; build up the costs to government, taxpayers, and even the industry itself; and prevent adjustments in domestic economies from occurring gradually and naturally. The political attractions of subsidies are clear in the short run; the economic costs in the long run are not as apparent. The efforts of the GATT and the OECD are essential to underline these costs in politically meaningful ways and to arrive at solutions to unrestrained competition between government treasuries in supporting exports.

NOTE

1. There have been numerous allegations that France, the major supporter of Airbus export activities, has used political pressures to sell aircraft; has granted landing rights in France to those airlines buying the Airbus; and has used predatory pricing and payoffs to ensure sales.

8 GOVERNMENT CARTELS

The director general of the GATT, Arthur Dunkel, said in 1982 that bilateralism and sectoralism are the "greatest present danger" to order and prosperity in the world (Dunkel 1982). Every bilateral trade deal between governments weakens the international system of trade rules. Every sectoral agreement arranges trade according to political pressures, not market forces. Every sector whose trade is managed by government loses some of its independence, its freedom of action, and becomes a ward of the state.

Most of the arguments made by trade policy experts and economists against sectoral trade agreements stress the protectionist nature of these agreements. They usually stem from the pressure of imports from aggressive exporting nations on markets historically served by domestic industries that are perhaps higher cost, and thus less competitive. In the classical world of free trade, such industries no longer enjoy comparative advantage and should decline.

This scenario fails to take into account the domestic political support that even declining industries may be able to generate if they are big enough and employ enough, or if they are critical to national defense. If one or more of those conditions is fulfilled, then the classical solution of substitution of imports for domestic production simply will not be allowed. The alternative solution in the trade-managed world is a limitation of one kind or another on imports, reached through government-to-government negotiations.

There are substantial grounds for the GATT director general's fears. Many examples of trade-limiting sectoral agreements exist. In some, governments are the major players because they are the traders of the commodities or goods. This group of agreements establishes "government cartels", which will be examined in this chapter. In other cases, the sectoral agreements are negotiated by governments, but imposed on private firms; they form the subject of the next chapter. All of these agreements limit trade; not one increases production, demand, or trade. Moreover, all have the effect of shifting economic burdens from stronger countries to weaker ones, or from parties to the agreement to those not party, precisely the results feared by the GATT.

If left unchecked the trend toward such agreements will not only cause the withering away of the GATT but also the disintegration of the international economic system. That is the real fear. The origins and operations of these sectoral arrangements and their impact on trade must be carefully examined if they are to be guarded against in the future. But my prediction is not a rosy one – the pressures are too strong and the temptations too great. I believe we will test the resiliency of the system much further before we are weaned from these facile and tempting "answers" to trade problems.

OIL AND OPEC'S TRADE MANAGEMENT

This analysis of sectoral trade management will begin with the biggest and most entrenched of the sector cartels, the Organization of Petroleum Exporting Countries (OPEC). OPEC has existed so long that people sometimes forget that it is nothing more than a cartel set up by the oil states to control the prices and production of the largest commodity in world trade, oil. Thus it satisfies the most important aspects of our definition of trade management – the conscious control or influencing of international trade for governmental purposes. Commodities are prime candidates for such control since normally there are few producers, inelastic or relatively constant demand, and significant "developmental" political overtones.

OPEC was formed in the early 1960s to coordinate the production and pricing policies of the major oil-exporting states. Before that time the oil companies, which owned the production and distribution facilities, bargained with individual countries and were able to keep oil country revenues at low levels. With the sharp increase in oil prices in 1973, immense discretionary surpluses became available to the Gulf and other oil producers. From 1974 through 1980, OPEC accumulated surplus reserves of $388 billion. Their revenues from oil exports were much more; this is the net figure left after all imports were paid for, and all other nondiscretionary expenditures were made. It represents the net new wealth of the OPEC states, almost all of which remained in governmental or royal family hands.

The investment of this enormous sum gave unprecedented control of large financial and industrial assets to a relatively small group of governments. By a combination of statesmanship and salesmanship on the part of industrial countries, about 85 percent of this discretionary investment was placed in the West—half in bank accounts ($154 billion) and the other half in portfolio investments in corporate and government securities. The remaining 15 percent was returned to non-OPEC developing countries through direct loans and grants (13 percent) and through the World Bank and the IMF (2 percent).[1] The oil exporters embarked on a development and investment binge of unprecedented magnitude.[2]

In the 1980s OPEC has faced a series of challenges. First, a number of non-OPEC oil producers have emerged, some of which themselves have become exporters. As a result, OPEC now accounts for only about 40 percent of world oil production. Even though it still accounts for over half of international trade in oil, OPEC will face other exporters in the market who are outside the cartel. For any cartel to be successful, it must control all, or substantially all, of the supply—a condition no longer fulfilled. Accordingly, OPEC will become more subject to market forces.

Second, as economic activity fell off during the worldwide recession in the 1980s, so did demand for energy, further crimping OPEC's exports. This revealed inherent conflicts among OPEC members, the most important of which led to the Iran–Iraq war. The fragile political consensus of the 1970s, which held the cartel together, is in danger of crumbling in the face of these conflicts.

OPEC may never again be in the same commanding position it held in the middle 1970s. After the partial oil embargo of 1973, OPEC not only controlled prices but forced the greatest wealth transfer in the history of the world. The stabilization of oil prices in the early 1980s, after a decade of relentless increases, is in great part due to the loosening of OPEC's grip on world oil production and distribution. Most recently, with the increases in Saudi and other production, prices have plummeted, demonstrating the close relationship between supply and price.

But there may be more resiliency in OPEC than first appears. There is a willingness of some countries, notably Saudi Arabia and Kuwait, to reduce drastically their production and revenues so as to allow others with larger populations and more urgent demands to continue to earn. This suggests an enlightened cartel management that may be able to weather the storm.

Regardless of the fate of OPEC, its importance is clear. It was able to cause almost singlehandedly a worldwide recession, through its rapid price escalation of a basic commodity essential to industrial economies. In the future it may be able to regain similar leverage, in spite of efforts since the gasoline shortages to conserve, to diversify sources of supply, and to encourage new non-OPEC production. The OPEC governments will not easily forgo any opportunity to exercise that leverage again. We can hope that OPEC will show more prudence now that the extent of its power is known and its stake in the health of the world economy is more direct — the dividends it cuts now will be its own.

Even though OPEC's ability to control oil trade may decline, its prominence in international finance and investment will not. The accumulated reserves, though not growing from oil revenues, have allowed the OPEC nations to ensure their role in international trade. Their wealth is now invested and earning; the loans to banks and developing countries have been made, and their own domestic development projects will begin to bear fruit. They will not grow as fast as they did in the boom period, but they will still be major influences on the world. This is the lesson of OPEC that other countries with commodities have tried to repeat, but without the success. There is no other commodity like oil in world trade, and no other cartel like OPEC.

COMMODITY AGREEMENTS

The principal distinguishing characteristic of OPEC is that it is a cartel, an organization of producers with a near monopoly acting together to control prices and production. OPEC has no oil consumers or importers in its membership. There is no comparable organization of oil importers, although the United States joined with other OECD developed countries to form the International Energy Agency in 1975. This is an attempt to counter some of the impact of oil boycotts, embargoes, and shortages. That agency does not manage the day-to-day oil business, however; it is strictly a standby arrangement, in case of supply interruption.

A class of trade agreements does exist that includes both suppliers and consumers. These agreements cover raw materials and commodities exported from tropical countries. They set quotas for exporters to reduce the competition between producers. In this way prices are intended to be stabilized, and production monitored and even regulated.

The economic arguments in favor of commodity agreements revolve around the price stability that supposedly results from the agreements. Stable prices smooth out producer incomes and enhance predictability. Agreements provide economic aid through transfer of wealth from richer purchasing countries to poorer supplier countries. This increases political and economic stability in producer countries, an obvious foreign policy interest of the United States. The problem is that no evidence supports these assertions. In fact, commodity agreements have quite different effects. Agreement-determined prices are usually too rigid to reflect market conditions, and thus they send wrong price signals to both consumers and suppliers. Inefficient producers are protected and new entrants are attracted, creating oversupply. High prices lead consumers to seek substitutes. The stocks held under the agreements (buffer stocks) are normally too small or too poorly capitalized to handle the swings in the market. And the bureaucratic and financial costs are often substantial (Wallis 1986).

International commodity agreements between governments were the only significant multilateral agreements concluded in the 1930s. They covered production and marketing of certain primary products. In some cases only producers were part of the agreement, in others both producer countries and consumer countries participated. Agreements on rubber (1934), tea (1933) and tin (1931) all evolved from private cartels. The coffee, sugar, copper, and wheat agreements stemmed from producer governments dealing with surplus production and unstable prices. All of these agreements covered 80 to 90 percent of the trade in their commodities. They did not have substantial impact on the commodity prices or volumes traded (except for tea, tin, and rubber) perhaps because there was already an industry predisposition to seek stability through a cartel (Kenwood and Lougheed 1983: 219-20).

The coffee agreement shows how the system works. The first agreement came into force in 1962 and was renewed in 1968 and 1976. The goals include the stabilization of markets and "long-term equilibrium" between suppliers and consumers (U.S. Department of State 1976). Its seventy-three members established an International Coffee Organization, with a ruling council and a board.

Each member who is an exporter of coffee is entitled to a quota, as agreed by the organization. For example, negotiations for quotas for the year beginning in October 1984 took place in April among the seventy-three members. The forty coffee-exporting countries who are members account for 99 percent of world shipments (58.2 million bags). Quotas are based on the 1976/77 shares of market, as modified in subsequent years. The agreement contains detailed provisions for the adjustment and use of these quotas.

As any good cartel attempts to do, the exporting members of the organization have raised the issue of controlling the exports from non-members. To be effective, a cartel must control most of the supply. The coffee organization attempts to do this by limiting the purchases of the importing countries, since it cannot control the nonmember exporters. Another concern is the shipment from members of coffee exceeding their quotas, a sort of black market in the world trade of coffee.

Policing the agreement requires constant surveillance of the "certificates of origin" required of exporting members. The coffee organization also sets daily "indicator prices" based on levels of production, inflation rates, consumption trends, changes in the world monetary system, and any other relevant factors. Since the coffee exporters have not agreed to adhere to those prices, they do not have the same effect as OPEC's posted prices, nor can they be enforced. Prices are nonetheless influenced, if not controlled indirectly, through the control of production.

The coffee agreement cannot control the weather or politics, and therefore its effectiveness is subject to conditions beyond its control. If a country has a bumper crop exceeding its allowed exports, the temptation to seek nonquota markets, selling at a discount, is great. This is especially true if coffee is the major foreign exchange earner. Conversely, if there is a drought, or other natural reduction in the crop, the agreement allows for the increase of indicator prices to account for the limited supply.

This limited control is the price the exporters must pay to keep the major importers within the agreement. Without their participation, the agreement would fall apart; there are too many suppliers, each capable of looking after its own interests. The developing country exporters would like to see a much tighter agreement that specifies required import quotas and prices, as well as export quotas. This would be a much more strictly managed system than the industrial importers want. The threat of departure of the major importers, such as the EEC or the United States, keeps the agreement as close to a market agreement as possible.

There are similar arrangements, with some differences in nuance, for jute, cocoa, sugar, tea, cotton, bananas, and hard fibers. Rubber and tin are also subject to agreements with similar provisions. All of these agreements are designed to alleviate the serious difficulties arising from surpluses or shortages and to achieve stable conditions in the trade of the specific commodity. With stability should come prosperity for producers; they can avoid the costs of excess production and the intense competition for export markets.

The record of these agreements has not been good. Few have lasted very long, and those that have do not substantially improve the production or price stability of the commodities controlled. The inherent difficulty is negotiating agreements that satisfy both producers and consumers. Each side is necessarily concerned with protecting its own interests, and those interests are in opposition.

As late as the 1970s and early 1980s, as part of the "new international economic order" being sought by the developing countries, the United Nations Conference on Trade and Development (UNCTAD) was still trying to promote the idea of commodity agreements and to finance the accumulation of the inventories (buffer stocks) required to control the markets through a "common fund" of $6 billion. The fund was created in 1979, but the resources devoted ($470 million) are much too small to do the job intended. The Reagan administration opposed the negotiation of more commodity agreements, and has limited the amount of money devoted to the common fund. It is likely that no further attempts will be made to negotiate other commodity agreements or additions to the fund in the near future.

There are certainly differences of opinion about the long-term impact of these agreements. Free market advocates see any agreement as intervening with market forces. Development economists see the agreements as dealing with the problem of unpredictable earnings, thus giving developing countries a chance to build more diverse economic bases. Whatever the long-term impact, they are just one more step along the road to a trade-managed world.

NOTES

1. See, for example, "OPEC Current and Capital Accounts" (1983), which reviews the revenues and expenditures of OPEC and the use of its surpluses.
2. As an example of the changes in attitudes accompanying oil wealth, I can cite one of my own experiences. During my first visit to Saudi Arabia as a development consultant in 1966, the country's plans were modest — the $15 million cost of building a new flour mill was considered extravagant. In contrast, as assistant secretary of commerce and a member of the U.S. delegation to the U.S.-Saudi Joint Economic Commission in 1981, I was briefed on Saudi's latest ventures to build two new industrial cities costing billions of dollars.

9 MANAGED SECTORS

This chapter will examine the three most important sectors in which governments manage trade: textiles, steel, and autos. These sectors have been at the root of the most bitter trade disputes, resulting in great dislocations in trade patterns. The disputes have persisted and will continue to characterize trade for the rest of this century.

Perhaps the largest step taken on the road to trade management was the Short-Term Arrangement (STA) on cotton textiles in 1961. The STA became the Long-Term Arrangement the following year and has continued, in one form or another, ever since. It now controls, in much more direct and binding ways, world trade in cotton, wool, and manmade fibers, and apparel made in developing countries. It is the most universal and most restrictive trade management system in the world today.

To understand how this arrangement originated, it is necessary to review a little history and to recognize the power of the textile and apparel industries. During the 1980 presidential campaign and transition, Senator Strom Thurmond of South Carolina, the premier textile state, induced then candidate Reagan to sign a letter promising to obtain tighter controls on textile imports if he were elected. During the transition, the industry came to call bearing the letter to remind those formulating the trade policies of the Reagan administration that they fully expected compliance with the bargain. Three years later they collected. How the free trade U.S. government has become an agent of a protectionist textile industry is a fascinating story that began in the nineteenth century.

With the exception of the United Kingdom and Japan, tariff protection of textiles has been commonplace from the nineteenth century to the present. During the interwar period, there was a great increase in protectionism as a result of Japanese exports and depression politics. The first known voluntary export agreement in textiles was concluded between the United States and Japan in 1936.

During the 1950s Japan began its extraordinary postwar export drive. From a base of $533 million in exports in 1949, it increased exports 600 percent to $3.4 billion a decade later. Since Japan was not a member of the GATT until 1955, many countries could discriminate against Japanese products without interference. Even after Japan joined the GATT, several countries maintained discriminatory policies, as exceptions under Article XXXV (which allows for nonapplication of the GATT if the countries have not bargained with each other).

As a result of a U.S. proposal that reflected an international concern with the export drive of Japan and of other developing low-wage countries, the GATT became involved. It issued a report in 1961 that identified the problem as "market disruption", resulting from excessive and rapid exports that threatened domestic industries. The GATT recommended consultations to arrive at constructive solutions, providing for "orderly expansion of international trade" and the protection of each member's legal rights.[1] The GATT members recommended forming a Permanent Working Group to hold these consultations and study the problem further (neither of which occurred).

Dam speculates that a prime reason for the lack of follow-up was Japan's own campaign to negotiate bilateral agreements to keep its export markets open in return for accepting certain limitations. In addition the United States in 1961 proposed a specific arrangement for cotton textiles — the most troublesome market disruption commodity.

The political impetus in the United States came from President Kennedy's election and his promises to help the textile industry. This industry felt the brunt of the low-wage exports and, like a large employer in any country, it wields substantial political power. Not only the United States but every European country leaped at the opportunity to protect its domestic industry. The result was quick agreement on the Short-Term Arrangement in 1961.

The present agreement is known as the Multi-Fiber Arrangement (MFA), and its scope is very broad. Four such arrangements have been negotiated, the latest in 1986. Since 1974 the MFA has controlled textiles and textile products of cotton, wool, and man-made fibers. The amount of trade controlled is substantial—about 30 percent of the manufactured exports of developing countries. The MFA sets a framework for bilateral agreements between each exporter of these products and each importer. The MFA establishes the overall objective of 6 percent annual growth in exports, and sets the terms and conditions under which this growth is to be achieved.

The 1981 renewal was the cause for a battle within the administration. The MFA is admittedly protectionist. Therefore, the economists in the Council of Economic Advisers, led by William Niskanen and aided by a devastating OECD analysis of the costs of protectionism, fought to eliminate (or at least loosen) the arrangement to allow more imports.

In the Reagan administration, issues that are not solved at lower levels are discussed at high-level White House meetings of the cabinet councils or their subsidiary committees. At a meeting of the Trade Policy Committee, economists argued that gutting the MFA would help the developing countries, save consumers' money, and slow inflation. Economic libertarians, opposed to any government intervention in the free markets, agreed. On the other side, the pragmatists in the administration merely pointed to the presidential commitment, the number of American jobs at stake, and the influential senators and congressmen who supported the arrangement and even sought to tighten it. The economists were quickly overruled and the MFA was renewed.

As a result of the renewal, the major importers negotiate bilaterally with the major exporters. In these negotiations specific limits are set for each product (e.g., men's wool sweaters) from each source (e.g., Hong Kong) to each destination (e.g., the United States). Moreover, the quota is monitored at both ends, with the exporter sharing with the importer the responsibility for enforcement. Whenever the imports get close to the level of the annual quota, the exporter is expected to stop exports, and the importer to stop further entries.

According to one observer, the United States has had effective constraints since the early 1970s, with more restrictive agreements negotiated during the late 1970s. This was also a period of expanding U.S. textile exports. The net effect was that total textile and apparel imports into the United States were actually lower in 1981 than in 1971, but imported clothing increased from less than 7 to 13 percent of U.S. consumption in the same period (Wolf 1983: 466).

The United States has entered into approximately twenty bilateral agreements since the renewal of the MFA in December 1981. The most important suppliers to the United States are Hong Kong, Korea, and Taiwan (the "big three") with about 40 percent of total imports. China has grown quickly to supply about 10 percent of U.S. imports. All of Latin America supplies slightly less than 10 percent with all other developing countries amounting to about 17 percent. Imports from Japan still account for 8 percent, but are declining; and as a developed country, Japan is no longer subject to restraints.

The EEC is the other major importer, and it has reached agreement with twenty-five countries since the MFA renewal. Its bilateral agreements allow for growth at about 1 percent less per annum than in the 1976–1981 period, in the categories posing the greatest competition for domestic producers. Actual reductions in quotas were negotiated with Hong Kong, Korea, and Macao, the dominant suppliers. The Community also sought to limit the flexibility of suppliers to shift from one category to another and to limit rapid increases — changes which would further restrict trade.

TEXTILE TRADE DISPUTES

The effects of these restrictions on the suppliers have varied over time. Japan's exports of textiles declined as it moved into higher value products. But for many newly industrializing countries, textiles and apparel are entry-level industries that are very attractive because of their substantially low-skill, low-wage employment. In 1981 and 1982 there was a concerted effort to curtail the growth allowed the "big three", to make room for new suppliers, including China.

But the most protectionist developments in textiles occurred in late 1983 and early 1984. When China thought it could take advantage of its growing political ties with the United States to expand its exports of apparel to the United States, it was taught a quick lesson in American politics. The textile and apparel industries employ 1.9 million in the United States, 800,000 more than the steel and auto industries combined.

First, the U.S. domestic industry filed a complaint alleging unfair competition based on Chinese subsidies to its apparel industries. Next, the textile lobby swung into action. Senate supporters (particularly Senators Helms of North Carolina and Thurmond of South Carolina) pressured the White House, citing among other arguments their reelection campaigns. At a White House drafting session in December 1983, just minutes before the industry's complaint was to be acted upon, the administration agreed to trigger import bans and new negotiations, not just with China but with all Third World suppliers. The action against China was thereby diluted at the cost of even further restrictions against all suppliers.

Consultations to revise agreements were called, and new quotas were imposed on the imports from thirty-two countries. The reaction from the exporters was swift; they accused the United States of protectionism and of violating its international agreements. They filed a formal complaint with the GATT, which has jurisdiction to review textile agreements. The textile sector thus triggered yet another foreign policy dispute; it has caused conflict ever since the first agreement in 1961.

And what has been the effect in the protected countries? Economists have calculated the costs of protectionism to consumers forced to pay higher prices for domestic products. One study of Canadian restraints showed that the cost to Canada was $430,000 in higher prices, social costs, and transfers to producers for each Canadian job protected in its textile and apparel industries. The total cost to Canadian consumers in 1979 was Can$467.4 million, of which tariffs cost Can$269.1 million and quotas cost another Can$198.3 million (Wolf 1983: 472, 477).

No more discriminatory and protectionist system could be imagined for handling trade. The so-called Short-Term Arrangement covering one product has grown into a permanent fixture of trade. It can be manipulated at will, by political forces and protected industries. The exporters themselves, by now, have learned to live with the system and even have a stake in its continuation.

By limiting the freedom of developing countries to move into these industries, the developed countries have essentially abandoned the concept of comparative advantage. They have also lost their credibility in advocating free market solutions to trade problems. As Martin Wolf of the London Trade Policy Research Centre pointedly argues, "What is the reality? It is that those who succeeded by market-oriented development and laud the idea of an open international system do not wish their words to be taken too literally by developing countries" (Wolf 1983: 456).

This section concludes with two important lessons. First, sectoral systems of discriminatory protectionism become more restrictive over time. This is the result of the political process motivating them. Every party is "bought off": the domestic producers with protection, the major exporters with access to markets that might otherwise be denied, and the minor exporters with the fruits of a government-imposed cartel that raises the prices they can charge. Consumers are too weak and disorganized to influence the process. In fact, in many countries the actions are invisible to the general public and are taken without public debate.

The second lesson is that selective actions like those authorized under the MFA will be used if available. Once the principle of nondiscrimination is abused or abandoned, as it has been in the textile trade, there is no longer any effective limit to discriminatory action. Successful protectionism breeds more protectionism. The result is a system based on coercion rather than rules. The danger of such a system should stand as a warning for those concerned with the two major sectors, steel and autos, now seeking similar protection.

MANAGEMENT OF STEEL TRADE

The current battle in trade management is over steel. The steel industry has contributed more than its share to the trade frictions of the 1970s and 1980s. But its future is still in doubt, and the solution to its many problems remains to be seen. The pattern established for steel will be indicative of the future of the entire international economic system, since it so concretely embodies all of the basic forces at work.

As one acute observer has noted, the industry

> ...finds itself in an unprecedented state of flux, with shifting competitive advantage and trade patterns among traditional suppliers, newly emerging export-oriented LDC mills, relatively stagnant demand, and stiff competition from other materials—all pointing to substantial market-driven structural adjustment in virtually every country involved in the industry (Walter 1983: 509).

The history and economics of the industry since the 1960s has received careful attention elsewhere and will not be duplicated here. However, a brief review of events prior to 1980 will reveal the groundwork for recent developments that have significantly influenced trade management.

By now the main actors and the scenario will be familiar. The United States steel industry suffered during the 1960s and 1970s from a host of problems. Wages were rising faster than productivity; technology was improving rapidly, but could only benefit those companies installing new mills; U.S. capital investment lagged behind that of other industries and countries; new safety and environmental standards imposed new costs; and finally, U.S. government policy did not address the industry's problems.

In contrast, the Japanese were building the largest and most efficient steel industry in the world. They were taking advantage of the latest technologies, low-cost labor, ocean-borne (thus low-cost) coal and ore supplies, and "administrative guidance" from MITI, which essentially eliminated interfirm competition in export markets. The EEC intervened directly in its industry, first to establish indicative prices; then to establish in 1976 an EEC-wide steel cartel, Eurofer; and finally, to mandate prices and production levels backed by generous subsidies for phasing out old plants and reducing capacity. These policies were developed by the European Community Commission, under the direction of the Commissioner for Industry, Belgian Viscount Davignon, a formidable debater and shrewd diplomat. Subsequently, the advanced developing countries — Korea, Taiwan, Mexico, Brazil, and later many others — built up their steel industries partly for export earnings. Thus during the 1960s and 1970s the stage was again set for trade intervention.

By 1968 the pressure on the U.S. steel industry from Japanese steel imports caused the United States to respond. First in a series of ad hoc solutions to trade problems was the voluntary restraint agreement (VRA). This agreement does not require admission of guilt on any part: The exporter may still claim it does not subsidize its exports or dump its product on the foreign market, and the importer does not need to show that its industry is hurt. But the VRA only temporarily solves the problem. The first agreement was negotiated between the United States and its major suppliers in Western Europe and Japan to limit the amount of steel exported from those countries to the United States. However, nothing actually was solved, then or now.

The first three-year agreement was renewed in 1972 for another three years. The Consumers Union filed a legal challenge, alleging that VRAs violated U.S. antitrust law, but the challenge failed. It did cast doubt on the validity of these arrangements, however; a doubt which still haunted policymakers a decade later.

As soon as the VRA expired in 1975, the steel workers sought relief from specialty steel imports. They filed a petition with the International Trade Commission (ITC) requesting, under section 201 of the 1974 Trade Act, to "escape" from the obligations of trade agreements (the escape clause action). The commission agreed that protection was warranted and recommended quotas on certain specialty steel products for a five-year period, to be negotiated with Japan and Europe. Japan formally agreed to the limits in an orderly marketing agreement (OMA)—a unilateral control of exports by the exporting country. Europe did not agree to an OMA, so the United States imposed import quotas for three years.

It is worth pointing out that the EEC itself has aggressively negotiated VRAs to protect its plan to support the domestic industry. In May 1977, when the reference prices were made mandatory under the Davignon Plan, imports into the EEC threatened to undercut the plan. In order to limit lower cost imports, VRAs were quickly negotiated with all other European steel producers outside the EEC, and with steel producers in Japan, South Africa, Spain, Korea, Australia, and with the East European suppliers of Poland, Hungary, Romania and Czechoslovakia.

One of the perennial fascinations and complications of trade is the interaction between countries. Not only bilateral trade flows must be considered but also activities between other countries. For instance, the Europeans had pressed Japan for an informal understanding in 1976 to reduce their exports to Europe, thus freeing product and putting pressure on the U.S. market. Again the steel workers pressed for relief, this time complaining to the U.S. trade representative of unfair trade practices on the part of the Japanese. That complaint was not accepted, but it led to other developments.

In February 1977 Gilmore Steel, a small West Coast producer, filed an antidumping suit against a few Japanese firms, alleging pricing under cost, or dumping product on the U.S. market. U.S. Steel and others followed by the end of the year, effectively swamping the Treasury Department (which at the time had the authority over such cases, before it was transferred to the Commerce Department in 1979).

To investigate, the Treasury Department requested cost information from the Japanese producers. The Japanese government preferred the possibility of another voluntary restraint agreement and withheld the information. Given the doubts about VRAs, and the Carter administration's wish to avoid negotiating bilateral trade restraints, the

Treasury went ahead with the investigation, found dumping, and assessed a 12 percent duty on Japanese imports.

A longer term solution was clearly desirable; dumping cases could be brought against any product from any country whenever it sold for less than the U.S. product. No exporting country could be assured of continued sales to the United States. The mechanism established by the Treasury in 1978 was ingenious: whenever sales occurred below the cost of the most efficient foreign producer (Japan) it was defined as dumping. All sales above that price were considered legal and would not be investigated, regardless of actual costs of production. Any sale below that price would trigger an antidumping investigation. This device was called the Trigger Price Mechanism (TPM). Thus the Europeans and the less efficient producers could sell steel in the United States even if it was actually being dumped.

It has been estimated that the TPM raised import prices about 10 percent in 1979. Domestic prices did not rise more than 1 percent because imports and domestic products were not fungible. Obviously the TPM was not a permanent solution to the dumping problem. It allowed high-cost European producers to continue to dump, increasing their market share. The TPM was revised in October 1980 (during the presidential campaign) as part of an assistance package for the steel industry. It increased the trigger price 12 percent, but this was not enough to slow the onslaught of imports. In 1981 imports climbed to 23 percent of U.S. sales, with prospects no brighter for the future.

CURRENT STEEL ISSUES

The Commerce Department in 1981 filed its own suit to challenge foreign subsidy practices. This investigation was underway when seven U.S. steel companies in February 1982 filed the largest trade suit in history against eleven countries' producers. The TPM was suspended since the suit had made it superfluous. The International Trade Commission again found injury, and the Commerce Department found subsidy in nine countries' exports (amounting to 20 percent of all U.S. imports).

Before the preliminary findings were finalized in October 1982, Commerce Secretary Malcolm Baldrige personally negotiated a solution with EEC Vice President Davignon. The groundwork had been laid during 1981 and 1982 in a series of meetings in Brussels (the home of the EEC) and in Washington. In the first meeting the possibility of a bilateral steel agreement was raised. Already the pressure of possible restraints on European exports of steel to the United States was beginning to unravel Davignon's carefully wrought plans in Europe to allow the orderly reduction of steel-making capacity. He claimed that continued, albeit reduced, access to the United States was crucial for the longer term solution of Europe's problems.

As the deadline for Commerce Department action approached, Baldrige was in daily consultation with Roderick, and the other steel executives and with Davignon to find a solution acceptable to both sides. The outcome of these negotiations was an orderly marketing arrangement limiting EEC sales in the covered products to about 5.1 percent of the U.S. market, down from 6 percent in 1981. As Secretary Baldrige remarked later, these were the toughest negotiations he had ever been involved in, either in government or in over thirty years in business.

Though the dispute between the United States and the EEC has been moved temporarily offstage, its effects are still being felt. The EEC immediately reduced the quotas for non-EEC suppliers to the Community. As the United States pulled out of the recession in 1983 and 1984, part of the growing U.S. demand was met by suppliers from the Third World. The industry realized the hydra has many heads, and to cut off one only reveals others. Its response has been even more direct, and on several fronts:

- It supports the Fair Trade in Steel bill imposing a flat 15 percent quota on all imports, a bill with more than 220 cosponsors in the House.
- It filed another round of cases based on unfair trading practices, winning a split decision at the International Trade Commission in favor of quotas.
- It lobbied heavily for quotas with the Reagan administration during the 1984 election campaign.

The result of the 1984 episode was a promise from President Reagan to negotiate more VRAs with the most significant suppliers to the U.S. market. The likely result of the ITC decision, and any others in the next few years, will be additional voluntary restraint agreements negotiated not only with the EEC but also with Japan, Brazil, Korea, Mexico, South Africa, and any other countries that attempt to penetrate the U.S. market in volume. There is no countervailing force opposing such agreements, since the most powerful consumer, the auto industry, is itself a proponent of these restraints.

One observer who has studied the industry closely, Professor Ingo Walter, concludes that some way of reducing the chaos is now necessary. He calls for a GATT-negotiated set of rules that incorporate safeguards against unwarranted unilateral action; consistency with the GATT Subsidies Code; a commitment to domestic adjustment of steel industries in developed countries (i.e., the United States and the EEC) to allow for Third World imports; better adherence to competitive practices by firms and labor; and short-lived tariffs, where necessary, to allow interim protection against sudden surges in imports (Walter 1983: 515). He defends this as preferable to continued attacks against the letter and spirit of the GATT, its codes, and its underlying principles.

A more sweeping solution is also possible. The industry itself argues for the certainty of quotas and protectionism. The ineluctable trend is toward some form of multilateral quota arrangement, like the textile MFA, the industry contends. And there is much to support this diagnosis. Partial solutions and ad hoc VRAs, OMAs, antidumping suits, and other actions will continue to plague the system during this period of transition and adjustment.

Steel is different, its supporters say, and it deserves special treatment. It is unique in the hierarchy of industries; it can lay claim to basic political support, which no other industry even approaches. As Walter says, "...the steel industry has shown a singular ability to penetrate institutions and achieve a telling impact on public policy. ...Governments have gone to great lengths to assure the proper legal and political frameworks within which the sectoral protection of steel can be realized" (Walter 1983: 509).

For these reasons an MFA for steel (a Multi-Ferrous Arrangement?) by 1995 would not be surprising. Indeed, an influential trade consultant and former deputy trade representative, Harald Malmgren, said recently that "My guess is that because of the serious industry restructuring going on, we'll slide into a multilateral steel agreement in the next few years whether or not policy makers want it" (*New York Times* 1984).

All of the conditions are right. The steps taken by the industry to force the agreement, combined with the existing network of bilateral restraints and the growth of new low-cost Third World suppliers all resemble the pre–Multi-Fiber Arrangement days of textiles. It is only a matter of time before this major step is taken toward more managed trade.

AUTOMOBILE TRADE

The last sector to be reviewed in this survey covers one of the largest industries in the world, automobiles. Throughout the world, most countries have some kind of auto manufacturing or auto assembly industry. As countries become more affluent and standards of living rise, automobile ownership rises to become a telling indicator. Government involvement in the industry includes protective tariffs for domestic assembly, government support for new investments, and government regulation of domestic content and exports. Auto companies buy, make, and sell worldwide.

The theory of comparative advantage argues that capital-intensive, high-skill industries should not be found dispersed but concentrated in countries like the United States. The Japanese have created comparative advantage in this industry, as in so many others, through use of advanced technologies, world-scale marketing and planning, production controls emphasizing cost and quality, and government support and protection.

Auto production has shifted accordingly to low-cost production centers, especially for small cars and for auto parts, such as engines and transmissions. U.S. firms are moving some of this production off-shore, investing abroad and developing integrated world car lines (Cohen 1983: 527). Combined with the already large share of the U.S. market represented by foreign, particularly Japanese, cars, there is great concern in the auto companies, unions, and auto states about the future of the U.S. auto industry.

As a result of these changes, the U.S. share of world auto production fell from 65 percent in 1965 to 20 percent in 1980. Japan's share increased from almost zero to 27 percent. Third World and other countries outside Europe rose from 2 to 15 percent. Western Europe became a net importer of cars. Imports rose as a proportion of the U.S. market from 3 percent in 1960 to 23 percent in 1980 (Cline 1983).

The automobile industry, because of its global reach, its extensive investments overseas, and its interlocking patent, sales, and dealer arrangements has long been among the most ardent free traders. In contrast to the steel industry, during the 1960s and 1970s both the auto industry and auto labor resisted the temptation to halt imports through government intervention.

This free trade stance came to an end in 1980, when the United Auto Workers (UAW), later joined by Ford, filed a petition with the International Trade Commission. The petition argued that the domestic industry was being injured as a result of the rapid rise in imports, and it sought relief in the form of quotas. The ITC found, in another split decision, that imports were not the major cause of the industry's problems; declining U.S. consumption of autos during 1979 and early 1980 was a more significant cause. Accordingly the complaint was dismissed.

After the 1980 election, President Reagan agreed to take another look at the problem. The losses of the auto companies had reached monumental proportions, with the U.S. makers recording cumulative deficits of $23 billion from 1978 to 1981. Imports continued to increase as a share of the market. At a cabinet meeting the president directed that a comprehensive program for the industry be developed under Transportation Secretary Drew Lewis. The program relied heavily on reducing the growth of imports through some form of agreement with the Japanese, in order to eliminate congressional pressure to legislate quotas.

THE VOLUNTARY RESTRAINT AGREEMENT

The U.S. Department of Commerce did not dispute the cost advantages enjoyed by Japanese producers who were able to deliver cars to the West Coast at $500 to $800 less than U.S. companies could. Nevertheless, the consumer shift to smaller cars looked more permanent than the companies had predicted, and the quality of Japanese cars was universally judged superior in consumer surveys. Investments by U.S. automakers were clearly warranted—in automation to reduce the cost gap, in quality control to improve consumer acceptance, and in new small car assembly lines. But the companies needed time and protection in order to make these investments.

This was the rationale for the negotiations with Japan in the spring of 1981 to put a cap on Japanese auto exports. The Department of Commerce judged it preferable to reach a three-year agreement allowing Japan to restrain its own exports, rather than to have legislation imposing mandatory quotas that could be impossible to remove. The president agreed and directed Ambassador Brock, the new U.S. trade representative, to negotiate such an agreement if possible.[2]

The negotiations leading to the voluntary restraint program in 1981 hit the heart of the Japanese export success. Automobiles, more than any other product, were viewed in Japan with immense pride. After all, its industry, in a short period of only two decades, had surpassed all of the European and most of the U.S. automakers. It was only because of severe quotas and enormous subsidies that any European autos were built, and the share of the U.S. market was growing rapidly each year. Moreover, the Japanese automobile makers were aggressive capitalists and free marketeers, just the sort of businesspeople the U.S. administration and the Japanese MITI bureaucrats seek to encourage.

Nevertheless the reality of quota legislation pending in Congress forced the issue. In a series of meetings with MITI officials, the United States argued that a three-year plan with reasonable restraints, set by the Japanese themselves, was vastly preferable to legislated quotas that the president could not promise to veto. The Japanese negotiator, Deputy Minister Amaya, a longtime MITI official widely respected for his wisdom and perception, agreed.

Amaya's job was to convince the auto industry to accept MITI's guidance. He met with U.S. negotiators during the day and with the automakers during the night for two days running to reach agreement. A polite courtesty call with the prime minister further underscored the importance of the issue. To continue the negotiations there was even a "secret" second dinner with Amaya one evening following a formal dinner announced to the press. At last agreement was reached and announced in the MITI minister's office with thirty or forty reporters and photographers recording the occasion.

The arrangement was a three-year limitation of auto exports from Japan to the United States set at 1.68 million cars for the first year, with opportunity for adjustment upward in subsequent years if U.S. auto demand and sales rose. The petition Ford filed with the ITC had requested a 1 million limit. Legislation pending in Congress contained a quota of 1.6 million per year for Japan. Clearly, the arrangement provided a higher limit than the industry, the unions, or the Congress wanted. It was not as high as the Japanese industry wanted, and the most difficult negotiations for MITI were with its own exporters. The exporters also had to bargain among themselves for shares of the U.S.

market, with the newer companies, like Honda and Suzuki, pitted against the giants, Toyota and Nissan.

When considering the U.S. response to the Japanese auto imports, it is important to keep in mind the actions of other countries with auto industries. Canada quickly negotiated its own agreement with Japan after the United States had succeeded. Canada even asked for U.S. help in the negotiations, as did Belgium in its negotiations with Japan. For years most of the EEC countries, acting individually, had imposed various barriers to limit imports: France imposed a flat 3 percent quota, the United Kingdom had an informal limit of about 10 percent, and Italy had the most stringent quota of all, a flat limit of 2,200 cars. In addition the EEC countries imposed a 10.9 percent tariff and various internal value-added taxes ranging from 13 percent (Germany) to 33 percent (France), compared with a 3 percent tariff in the United States and no value-added taxes. The Japanese face much higher barriers in Europe and other producing countries than in the United States.

The auto agreement has come under attack since it was negotiated, largely because of its success. It has limited Japanese imports in a rising market, allowing U.S. companies not only to sell but to charge premiums. Analysts estimate the costs of U.S. cars today may be $1000 higher than they would have been in the absence of the restraints. This had led to a much healthier industry, record profits, and substantial new investment, just as expected. Because of those record profits, the administration was opposed to continuation of the restraint after its fourth year, but it was nevertheless extended by the Japanese.

Continuing protection for the industry is a different matter. The UAW has backed legislation in several Congresses to impose local-content requirements on all autos sold in the United States. This would mean that for large-volume sellers like Toyota and Nissan, up to 90 percent of the content of the car in parts and labor would have to come from the United States. This would effectively ban large-volume imports and require investment in production and assembly in the United States.

The UAW estimates 800,000 jobs in auto plants, and auto parts plants would be saved. But the Council of Economic Advisers and others estimate the jobs saved would be more than offset by losses in import dealerships, by increases in the cost of living, and by trade losses in other sectors as a result of Japanese retaliation (Cohen 1983:

534). Secretary Baldrige called the local-content legislation the worst protectionist bill ever introduced in Congress. Presidential candidate Walter Mondale was the only one, Democrat or Republican, in the 1984 primaries or the general election, to support the bill. The bill did not pass during the election year and is unlikely to succeed in the near future.

The pressures for auto protection in the United States may diminish, first in the companies because of their global outlook, then in the auto unions as their jobs appear more secure, and lastly in Congress when the issue is no longer politically popular. "Jap bashing" has become a favorite pastime of auto state congressmen and politicians looking for an easy target for all U.S. ills.

But a change may be occurring. The U.S. companies have demonstrated their ability to compete, confounding their many critics. Lee Iaccoca has become a folk hero for turning Chrysler around, repaying the government-guaranteed loans ahead of schedule, and leading the company to its best years ever. New models and innovation have improved the product in the showroom and customers are buying. Surely, Japanese imports will continue their march upward in market share, but not at the destruction of the U.S. industry.

For these reasons, there seems little likelihood of either domestic-content legislation or an international protectionist agreement along the lines of the MFA in autos, as seems likely in steel. Nevertheless, developing countries will probably do everything in their power to limit imports into their markets, to develop their domestic industries, and to seek investment in the parts and component industries. Many of these investments will be made by U.S. companies to supply the U.S. market, thus continuing the relentless internationalization of the industry. In other words, this may be one sector that escapes the fate awaiting many others in the trade-managed world.

NOTES

1. Dam (1970: 298) quoting from the results of the working party set up by the contracting parties in 1959 to study the question.
2. I was able to join Ambassador Brock in Tokyo for the round of talks with the MITI minister and his officials to agree on the details of the arrangement.

10 THE INVISIBLE SECTORS

To complete this survey of trade relations in particular sectors, consider next the diverse activities under the heading of "invisibles"—services, investment income, royalties, management fees, and other sources of payments for which no merchandise has changed hands. This group of industries and activities is one of the fastest growing, most regulated, and least understood in the international economy. It is estimated that this group accounts for about one-fifth of world trade.

The first problem is one of simple definition. Certain categories of invisibles are well-known, familiar to international traders and economists alike. For example, any payment made to a shipping company for freight, or to an insurance company for coverage, is an invisible import if the ship or the insurer is foreign. Conversely, if McDonalds franchises a chain of fast-food shops in Japan (as it already has done successfully), then the franchise fee paid to McDonalds is for an invisible export of goodwill, management services, and other services. The first group of payments shows in the balance of payments as outflow, the second as inflow.

But the general concept of service industries is not as well defined. One way to proceed is first to identify all mining, manufacturing, and agricultural industries, and then define everything else as services. Another approach is to look at products: If the product is intangible, then the industry is a service. Compounding the problem is the lack of a standard definition for international statistical purposes. The Soviet Union distinguishes *productive services,* such as transportation of goods, from *nonmaterial services,* such as passenger transportation and all other services that only redistribute wealth (Shelp 1981: 41). And what about services and other sources of invisible income exported by manufacturing firms and classified elsewhere? These invisible exports are not separately accounted for in the U.S. balance of payments statistics.

The result of these definitional and accounting problems is that no one knows the extent of invisible trade flows between countries. Even U.S. statistics are woefully inadequate and legislation has been introduced and strongly supported to improve U.S. services data. Domestic accounts are slightly better than accounts with other countries, but neither set of data measures the true importance of services to the U.S. economy.

In his review of trade in invisibles, one observer points out that "...the countries most dependent on service exports include the United States, various West European countries, and several developing countries — Argentina, Korea, Egypt, and Iran. For these countries invisibles accounted for about 26 percent of their trade" (Shelp 1981: 40). In terms of magnitude, the United States is the biggest earner of invisibles income, accounting for almost 20 percent of the world total in 1978. France accounts for a little over 9 percent, then the United Kingdom and West Germany with almost 9 percent each, followed by Japan, Italy, and Belgium/Luxembourg (all around 5 percent, each) followed by the Netherlands, Switzerland, and Spain. All of the top ten are OECD members (Shelp 1981: 24).

In the ranking of the world's services earners, the first non-OECD country to appear is Saudi Arabia with about 2 percent of the world's services trade, primarily from crude oil shipping. The next developing countries to appear on the list are Korea and Mexico with about 1.2 percent each. The next largest are Singapore (1 percent), Iran (1 percent), and Egypt (almost 1 percent). These statistics give credence to the claims of the developing countries that there has been historically a concentration of services, a situation that must be changed. It is worth noting that the magnitude of exports of services does not correlate directly with domestic consumption; some countries with large domestic service sectors are not major exporters, and vice versa.

Developing countries have not yet fully realized the potential of services for their economies. Shelp states that ". . . while there is often but a limited awareness in developing nations of their potential for earning foreign exchange, with the primary focus being on tourism and, to a lesser extent, on shipping, there is a high level of consciousness of the need to limit service imports" (Shelp 1981: 78). This helps to explain the actions of Third World nations, which place barriers on the imports of services, stimulate domestic service firms in competition with foreign firms, and favor domestic firms over foreign ones wherever possible. The Third World's impetus for these restrictive moves often originates in the United Nations Conference on Trade and Development (UNCTAD) committees and codes.[1]

Nevertheless the UN study of the future of invisibles trade concludes that the developed countries will actually increase their share of world trade in services through the year 2000. This study, conducted by Leontief using input-output techniques, also forecasts that developing countries will reduce their share and the nonmarket economies will remain about the same (Shelp 1981: 71).

The current attention given to invisibles is indicative of both the emergence of new services, such as those stemming from the computer and telecommunications industries, and the neglect of already established services. U.S. trade legislation has authorized services negotiations, but these have not yet been attempted. Even U.S. tax deferral under the Domestic International Sales Corporations device has been limited. The Export-Import Bank has limited its support to services related to merchandise transactions. One bright spot has been the U.S. Overseas Private Investment Corporation, which has insured some services exports in connection with U.S. investments in developing countries.

GOVERNMENT PROTECTION OF SERVICE INDUSTRIES

The problems that must be addressed are even more varied than the service industries themselves.

> The central problems in services are the denial of right to establishment and, once established, burdensome licensing and certification requirements, limits on the range of services that may be provided, requirements

on nationality of employees, limits on foreign equity, and discrimination in government contracts, as well as more restrictive licenses and higher fees than for national firms (Cline 1983: 43).

In attempting to categorize the variety of problems, the U.S. Chamber of Commerce's Committee on Services, working with the Office of the U.S. Trade Representative, developed a list that indicates the scope of barriers service firms face:

1. Legal establishment
2. Local purchasing requirements
3. Marketing and selling
4. Access to public sector markets
5. Personnel
6. Foreign government regulatory procedures

Since all of these restrictions are government imposed, the range of control and intervention is broad. Governments may, in fact, manage service sectors even more than merchandise sectors.

Some of these restrictions require a more detailed explanation, beginning with legal establishment. Many countries deny access to the market by outright prohibition of service imports. Since the GATT does not deal with services, there is no violation of its provisions. Local operations, through the establishment of a subsidiary or other activity, may also be prohibited. Limitations may be placed on investments allowed in service firms; or even where they are allowed, there may be requirements to have local equity investors. In these industries, the ability to use personnel effectively is critical, yet many countries impose quotas or other limitations on employment such as requiring the use of local suppliers or subcontractors. Finally, marketing to both government and private customers may be severely limited, especially to the former.

Even if establishment of a subsidiary is allowed, personnel hired, and marketing permitted, heavy government regulation may still work against the foreign service provider. In some cases, there is little realization of the potential importance of service imports. In other cases, governments simply discriminate through their domestic regulatory processes, with unintended effects on foreign providers. As Shelp points out,

In the past the only government policies that were directed toward services usually dealt with their regulation. They have tended, for example, to make such industries as shipping and aviation noncompetitive and oligopolistic in their international pricing. The effect of this governmental control of key international services is to isolate them from other economic activities and exclude them from the traditional international commercial institutions (Shelp 1981: 76).

GOVERNMENT AS PROVIDER OF SERVICES

In many countries the government itself is the major provider of services. This is a powerful incentive to use the government's sovereign rights to protect its competitive position. Where the government owns the only national airline, for example, it will be extremely reluctant to jeopardize its investment in expensive aircraft and its foreign exchange earnings. For this reason the domestic routes will of course be closed to foreign competition. But even foreign routes may be carefully negotiated to limit competition and ensure a fair share of the revenues flow to the national carrier.

Some governments will go even further. While the United States since the end of World War II has pushed for equality of opportunity in international aviation under bilateral aviation agreements, most of its trading partners have sought the comfort of equality of results. Their airline routes are carefully balanced so that the national airline matches foreign airlines flight for flight. In some cases the revenues are split equally to ensure equality of results. Thus a passenger flying between Paris and Geneva, whether he goes on Air France or Swissair, generates equal amounts of revenue for each airline.

Pooling agreements that call for sharing of trade or revenues are used widely outside the United States. The London to Bombay shipping conference, for example, is open only to shipping lines of the United Kingdom and India. Shipping lines from other countries will be excluded from the conference. If they try to operate independently, the British and Indian governments will refuse to allow them to be served, the conference will undercut their prices to drive them off the market, or both. Similar arrangements exist in telecommunications, where traffic between countries is shared by the national government monopolies.

The United States has insisted that such pooling agreements are anticompetitive and has limited their use in U.S. commerce. The United States has required open conferences, which any shipping line may join. For instance, the North Pacific conference operating between

San Francisco and Tokyo is open to any shipping line from any nation. Similarly in communications, deregulation of the domestic industry has opened up to foreign competition opportunities for suppliers of a wide range of telecommunications equipment and services. International services are now provided by a variety of companies.[2]

IMPROVING THE SERVICES TRADE ENVIRONMENT

Substantial obstacles lie ahead in attempting to negotiate liberalization in services. Part of the problem lies in the entrenched attitudes of governments protecting their service industries. Another part of the problem is the web of specialized bilateral, multilateral, and general agreements developed through decades of painstaking work. Though the results of these agreements are not liked in all cases, they exist nevertheless. They represent accommodation and compromise for all countries involved. It is naïve to suggest that liberalization of service industries is just around the corner.

In recognition of these difficulties, two thoughtful observers of the services scene have wisely set out the questions that must be addressed before any meaningful negotiations begin (see Diebold, Jr. and Stalson 1983). The first question arises over goals — what are we trying to achieve? The basic principle of nondiscrimination in trade, underlying the GATT, may not be fully meaningful or achievable in services. Even if nondiscrimination or equality were attainable, it might not be desirable in every case. A foreign service provider may enjoy special or privileged status under law, which it would be loathe to give up. For example, until recent changes in U.S. law, foreign banks operating in the United States could open offices in all fifty states, while U.S. banks were restricted to their home state. Furthermore, discrimination in service professions can lie in immigration policies also, a sensitive area not normally broached in trade negotiations.

Another issue to be addressed is the nature of the bargain to be made in any trade negotiation. Would there be sufficient reciprocity in the undertakings to justify a multilateral negotiation? In the past, in industries such as aviation and shipping, the only feasible means of negotiating has been bilateral. Exchanging access to service markets immediately raises questions about the scope of opportunity. The huge U.S. market would then be compared to, say, the size of the

Argentine or Korean or Kuwait market. Conversely, the power, resources, and international experience of U.S. service providers would be compared with those of domestic firms, and protectionist instincts might be revived.

The long-term U.S. goal, as stated by U.S. Trade Representative Ambassador Brock, is "to negotiate a services code in the GATT that will incorporate a set of general rules and principles that govern trade in all service industries. Additionally, they would establish mechanisms for discussing issues and solving disputes following procedures already established by the GATT" (U.S. Congress 1982).

This goal was placed before the GATT ministerial meeting at the end of 1982, at the insistence of the United States. There was support from a few other delegations, including the United Kingdom, which is a traditional service exporter. The outcome of the ministerial was to begin a study of the existing barriers to services exports. While not great progress, at least it was a beginning.

It is worth considering some other suggestions of approaches to encourage services trade liberalization. For example, trade cases involving those services that are linked to trade in goods could be brought to the GATT. Or it might be argued that if a practice violates the GATT, then that same practice in services trade also violates the GATT. Both approaches would start the healthy process of deciding service trade cases in GATT. A third approach would use the concept of unfair trading practice, now found in U.S. law (section 301 of the Trade Act of 1974) to seek elimination of objectionable foreign practices (Diebold, Jr. and Stalson 1983).

These approaches seem doomed to failure. There is no doubt among GATT members that services are outside the GATT, a point made repeatedly by U.S. as well as other delegations to the 1982 ministerial meeting. Those who oppose new initiatives in the GATT tend toward an excessively legalistic treatment of the General Agreement. It is unlikely that any services issues will be decided in the GATT before specialized services codes are negotiated. Even those codes probably will be limited in scope and will not solve all service sector problems. They would only deal with those ripe for multilateral solutions.

In the meantime a moratorium on new barriers to trade in services is worth exploring. Even with exceptions and provisos to deal with local and special situations, such an agreement would be better than nothing. During the lengthy process of building a consensus for multilateral agreements, Diebold and Stalson recommend conducting bilateral discussions to remove specific barriers.

As part of this process, they counsel using U.S. legal recourse, including retaliation, to improve negotiating positions and to achieve results.

> There may be times when retaliation against foreign restrictive practices in services will be the best course and when some degree of reciprocity will be a reasonable formula for arranging the mutual removal of restrictions, but it should be an aim of foreign economic policy to keep these cases to a minimum and then to test in a tough-minded way the costs and benefits of such a course for the general national interest of the United States (Diebold, Jr. and Stalson 1983: 608).

Selective reciprocity may very well be the key to unlocking progress in this difficult area.

INVESTMENT RESTRICTIONS

National restrictions on foreign investment is related to services in several ways:

- Both flows are recorded in the invisibles accounts.
- Both have problems of definition and accounting.
- Both are outside the GATT.
- Both are important foreign exchange earners of developed countries, especially the United States.
- Both are heavily controlled by governments.
- Both are future battlegrounds in international economic policy.

Investment flows occur in wide variety, including direct investments, portfolio investments, short-term financial placements, interest payments, dividends, royalties, fees for management or services, franchising fees, lease payments, and rents. The focus here is on those aspects of government involvement in determining investment flows and the flows of products resulting from investment, the so-called trade-related investment problems.

In describing these problems, noteworthy again is the absence of agreed international rules. The GATT does not cover all trade-related investment problems, to say nothing of those unrelated to trade. The OECD has negotiated some nonbinding codes that set out principles to be followed, but these codes do not impose obligations on their signatories. Thus every country is free to discriminate against foreign investment, to prohibit it, or to regulate it without running afoul of any international agreement.

As a way of getting around this absence of rules, the United States has developed the concept of trade-related investment. This allows recourse to the GATT for specific complaints. In one recent and important case brought before the GATT by the United States, the Canadian Foreign Investment Review Agency was challenged. The United States sought relief on the general ground that it imposed conditions on those investments to restrict imports and stimulate exports. The conditions imposed ran the gamut of potential government interference with private decisionmaking. They included local hiring requirements, local purchasing requirements, export requirements, and commitments to future growth and employment.

The GATT would not address these issues. Instead the panel limited its decision, finding only that the Canadian requirement to purchase locally discriminated against foreign suppliers. In the GATT's view, all other conditions imposed were legal. The United States had also raised the same issues in the OECD Investment Committee to no avail, largely because almost all other countries impose similar conditions or wish to retain the freedom to do so.

Canada had to defend itself because it was straightforward about its policies. It had created an agency with an explicit charter to impose investment conditions, thus making the target easier to identify. In contrast, most other developed OECD countries are not nearly as obvious. Instead they use other, less visible, means to achieve the same ends (less "transparent", in the language of the GATT). In this area, countries prefer to deal with investors on a case-by-case basis, striking individual bargains. Reliable information about investment requirements is therefore hard to elicit and somewhat anecdotal, but suitable for GATT purposes.[3]

First to be examined are performance requirements placed on foreign investors before they are allowed to invest. These come in a variety of forms, such as setting minimum export or maximum import levels, specifying levels of domestic purchases of goods and services (domestic content), requiring technology of a certain level or type to be transferred, setting employment targets, and restricting foreign exchange transactions. Nations have imposed these requirements in the obvious attempt to get the most out of foreign investment. In the words of one investigator, they "...tend to shift production and re-lated investment and jobs from other countries. A requirement that exports be a given percentage of production or a minimum volume has the same effect as an export subsidy, since it raises exports beyond what they would otherwise be" (Safarian 1983: 613).

In a survey of U.S. companies, the U.S. Department of Commerce found that about 14 percent of the 23,641 reporting nonbank affiliates in foreign countries were subject to performance requirements in 1977 or before. Those investing in developing countries, particularly Latin America, reported significantly higher incidence at 29 percent of the sample. Developed countries imposed performance requirements only 6 percent of the time. In more than one-third of the total number of cases, the requirement was placed only on foreign firms.

National treatment, expropriation, and compensation for expro-priation are thorny issues. Since the general rule of law in this area is underdeveloped, the United States has relied on a century of bilateral treaties of friendship, commerce, and navigation (the FCN treaties) with over 50 countries. These define in the broadest terms possible the treatment to be accorded foreign investors in the United States and U.S. investors abroad.

The most common form of agreement is national treatment, mean-ing that a U.S. company will be treated the same in the foreign country as its own companies will be. An alternative, less stringent standard is most-favored nation treatment, meaning that the U.S. firm will be treated the same as the best treatment given to other foreigners. Clearly the first would prohibit discrimination while the second allows it. But the problem is the reach of either provision when dealing with pro-tected sectors, national security–sensitive industries, government mo-nopolies, or other exceptions.

Most governments abroad, and every state in the United States, offer incentives to investors. About 26 percent of U.S. companies investing abroad and reporting in the 1977 survey received some investment benefit. Sometimes incentives are offered to entice any investment; sometimes they are targeted to specific industries such as high tech-nology; sometimes they are limited to certain less developed regions (such as the south of Italy or the rural areas of Mexico); and some-times they are only offered to certain desirable investors. The incen-tives fall into three general categories: direct financial assistance, fiscal or tax assistance, and what I call "factor" assistance, which is related to particular inputs like labor, transportation, electricity, and land.

Investors and their host governments often collaborate to discriminate against noninvestors. A major variable of interest to investors is the tariff schedule. Investors seek reduced tariffs for the machinery and equipment that they are importing for any new plant. Perhaps more important, they also seek protection from further imports of the products to be made. This is a powerful encouragement to investment, but it is also directly contrary to GATT rules. The practice is justified in the case of developing countries by the argument that their infant industries require this kind of protection to be viable.

The investor often agrees to meet certain goals in order to qualify for the incentive. There is frequently a direct link between the incentive and the performance requirement. It could be argued that such goals are not really requirements but rather the quid pro quo for government assistance. The investor is theoretically free to forgo the incentive and ignore the goals. In practice, however, this option may not be available. The requirements may be imposed anyway, and the investment may not make sense unless the higher costs of factor inputs are offset by the subsidies, or the competitors are benefiting from the incentives. An investment would not be feasible without the incentives; performance requirements are just part of the deal.

In most foreign countries incoming investors must receive government approval of their investment plans. They are also required to report on their progress in meeting the imposed goals. Before any profits can be sent out of most developing countries or nonmarket countries, the investor must normally receive approval to buy and transfer foreign exchange. Since this approval can be denied without legal recourse (on the grounds of overriding shortage of foreign currency, for example) the prudent foreign investor keeps a clean record and a low profile, and tries to stay on the best possible side of the ruling party, class, or clique. He is not likely to complain loudly, go to court, or even seek U.S. government intervention in an investment dispute, except as a last resort. This gives most foreign governments, even in developed countries, a strong hand when dealing with the supposedly elusive and powerful multinational corporation.

In order to deal with expropriation of U.S. investments in foreign countries, the United States pursues several different tacks. Through the Overseas Private Investment Corporation (OPIC), a semi-independent federal agency, it offers protection against several types of risk inherent in doing business abroad—expropriation, war, and even certain kinds of commercial risks. By its charter OPIC focuses its programs on developing countries and is an effective stimulus to U.S. investment in those countries. To signify its importance as a development agency, the administrator of the Agency for International Development serves as OPIC's chairman, and its policies are closely monitored by the State Department as well as the Treasury and Commerce Departments.

In its approach to some of the problems occurring between U.S. investors and their host governments, the Reagan administration began in earnest the negotiation of bilateral investment treaties (BITs) to go beyond the generalities of the FCN treaties. The BITS specify the treatment to be accorded by each country to the investors of the other; the terms of entry; protection against expropriation; and the procedures for settling disputes. These treaties go a long way toward filling the gaps in the international trade system resulting from the absence of any international agreements covering investment.

There have been nine bilateral investment treaties negotiated thus far with developing countries (Egypt, Panama, Morocco, Zaire, Turkey, Cameroons, Haiti, Senegal, and Bangladesh) and a number are under discussion, including important ones with China and Malaysia. All signs are that these treaties will continue to gain popularity as more developing countries realize the benefits of direct foreign investment without strings, conditions, anti-multinational corporation rhetoric, or Third World posturing. The BITs are not a substitute for more general, universal solutions to investment problems, but they offer much greater protection for U.S. investors in the absence of broader solutions. They should be pursued.

NOTES

1. In an earlier work, I dealt extensively with the role of UNCTAD and other intergovernmental agencies in developing restrictive codes (see Waldmann 1979a).
2. These few examples are drawn from my own experiences as a negotiator when I was deputy assistant secretary for transportation and telecommunications in the U.S. Department of State.
3. In several previous works I have catalogued the incentives and restrictions applicable to foreign investors (see Waldmann and Mansbach 1978; Waldmann 1979b; Waldmann and Cohn 1984).

11 EAST–WEST TRADE

Since the October Revolution in 1917, trade relations between the Soviet Union and the West have been subject to the pervasive conflict between the capitalist and communist systems. Since World War II, trade has become an informal barometer, used by both sides to measure the state of relations. More important, both sides have used trade as a weapon in conducting the relentless cold war between East and West, a war that appears to have no end.

Both East and West rely on government direction of trade to improve political relationships, but the West has neither the capacity nor the instruments to control trade as thoroughly as does the East. The Soviets control every product and technology imported into or exported from the East bloc, so any trade that takes place occurs within an already restricted area. Within the Soviet system the goal pursued by that control is political and military, regardless of the rhetoric that surrounds it.

As N. V. Zinoviev, head of the Department of Trade with the Americas of the Soviet Foreign Trade Ministry said,

It would be naive to suggest that trade and politics are not interdependent. Political relations provide a climate for the development of trade relations but trade, in its turn, being sufficiently developed, has the effect of "reverse impact" on political relations, influencing them in a positive way, helping to stabilize them (Zinoviev 1983: 6).

East bloc control of trade provides the clearest example of government management of trade contrary to the principles of free trade. It also reflects the insidious and debilitating results of such management. Even in the areas where trade is permitted, the Soviet government owns the means of production and the agencies of international trade. Also, trade among the East bloc countries is managed according to plan, thus further diminishing the area of open trade and increasing the proportion of world trade managed by governments.

The failures of the East bloc's planned economies result in some measure from the rigidities and inflexibilities of its trading regimes. It is only by getting out from under those regimes that countries like Yugoslavia and Hungary, and to a lesser extent Romania and Poland, have been able to approximate Western growth and dynamism. Cuba adopted East bloc methods and has stagnated for twenty-five years. China today realizes the mistakes of the past and is experimenting desperately with unorthodox, nonsocialist ways to develop rapidly.

EXPORT CONTROLS

East–West trade is controlled by the West for a variety of reasons. The potential for nuclear war carries overriding importance. National security has dictated a direct and intimate involvement of the United States and allied NATO governments in controlling sales of weapons, technology, and productive facilities useful for military purposes to the Soviet Union and its allies.

Most countries will prohibit normal commercial relations with the enemy during wartime. So the U.S. Trading with the Enemy Act, which has provisions restricting financial dealings, travel, and other normal relationships during a time of war, is not unusual. But extending the concept to restrictions on trade with potential enemies, as opposed to actual ones, raises questions of public policy. The conclusion reached by the U.S. and other NATO governments is that such trade should be restricted; but this is not fully accepted by the U.S. business community or by all trading partners of the United States.

The Export Administration Act provides the framework for those peacetime restrictions in the United States. The control program following World War II totally embargoed exports to Communist nations, but it quickly became clear that broader efforts were necessary. The 1949 act prohibited exports that threatened U.S. national security, regardless of destination. This applied to not only all sales to the Soviet Union and the Eastern European satellite countries but also sales to any other country through which goods could flow or be diverted to embargoed countries. Thus the full-blown control system in use today evolved, with complete monitoring of exports to any country.

For some time, exports of items in short supply in the United States have been prevented. In addition, the United States controls the export of munitions and other defense equipment to all destinations under a separate statute administered by the Departments of State and Defense. The ability to reward the defense ministries of its friends and deny weapons to those of its foes forms a basic instrument of U.S. foreign policy. Export controls can also prevent doing business with countries harboring terrorists or committing gross violations of human rights.

Since 1979 the law has contained a separate authority for controls on exports for foreign policy (as distinct from national security) purposes. These controls are imposed by the president to indicate displeasure with foreign governments and to influence foreign behavior. They were imposed on the Soviet Union after the Afghanistan invasion and the Polish military takeover, and on Iran after the taking of the hostages, to mention two recent targets.

The Trading with the Enemy Act itself placed some limits on the exercise of foreign policy controls, but Congress wisely refrained from intruding too far into the process, knowing that it is impossible to foresee all situations. Because of the amount of discretion involved, these controls spark controversy in the U.S. business community and Congress. Export controls still remain one of the president's few options between sending a diplomatic protest note and sending in the marines.

The core of U.S. export controls, however, continues to be the basic national security provisions. No one objects to the concept of denying weapons to adversaries of the United States, but beyond that, disagreements abound. Does this mean at all times, or only when the environment is hostile? Does this mean only the instruments of war, or also the capacity to make them? Does it extend to any help to the adversary's economy, even to exports of grain or other food? And if technology is controlled, does this extend to contacts between researchers, academics, and others not actually employed by exporters?

Some of the most difficult questions arise when the U.S. control program and those of its allies do not control the same things. Partial coordination is achieved through COCOM, the coordinating committee of the NATO countries. COCOM maintains a list of products and technologies that the Western allies have agreed not to sell to the East bloc. COCOM also considers exemptions to the general ban on exporting whenever one country seeks an exception. There are periodic reviews of the control list, including one completed in 1984 at the request of the Reagan administration.

But what if allies of the United States do not agree with the U.S. conclusion that control of a particular product (e.g., a computer) is vital to Western national security, and they attempt to sell to the East? What action should the United States take? Should it deny these allies or the offending foreign firms the right to export to the United States? And what about sales to U.S. allies and subsidiaries of U.S. companies abroad—the so-called West–West trade? Should the same time-consuming process to get an export license apply as for East–West trade?

THE PIPELINE CRISIS

Part of the difficulty the U.S. Congress faced in renewing the Export Administration Act stemmed from the Polish military takeover at the end of 1981 and U.S. actions in response. The Polish military, with Soviet support, imposed martial law in December 1981 to crack down on the Solidarity labor movement. To indicate U.S. displeasure, President Reagan directed the administration's senior officials to develop a program of retaliatory actions. Export controls unquestionably formed part of the program, but hard-liners in the administration saw an opportunity to win a victory that heretofore had eluded them—the slowdown or halt to construction of the Soviet gas pipeline to Western Europe. The controls, therefore, specifically embargoed sales to the Soviet Union of U.S. oil and gas equipment or technology, and the products of U.S. technology manufactured abroad.

The problem arose when European allies of the United States objected, particularly those that were scheduled to receive the Soviet gas and thus had been selling pipeline equipment to the Soviets. They pointed out that the Carter administration had failed to object to the pipeline. Furthermore, during 1981 the allies had fended off several attempts of the Reagan administration in NATO, at the OECD, and even at the summit of the leaders of the seven industrial countries to stop the pipeline. Using the Polish crisis as a pretext did not seem fair to the British, French, Italian, and German firms or their governments. They all visited Washington to argue their case.

One of the foreign companies planning to ship pipeline equipment was the subsidairy of a U.S. company, and others were licensees of General Electric in the United States and thus subject to export controls. The U.S. government considered that its jurisdiction and its export controls extended to those companies. The issue became critical when the British and French governments disagreed that U.S. jurisdiction extended that far. They ordered their companies to ship compressor parts to the Soviet Union for the pipeline.

The U.S. response was to restrict the rights of those companies to use U.S.-licensed technology elsewhere. Through the summer of 1982, barbs were exchanged across the Atlantic about "trade wars," "the worst crisis in the alliance," and similar rhetoric. There were signs that actions were about to be taken, but they were forestalled by Secretary of State George Shultz, who negotiated a "ceasefire" in the fall of 1982. The Europeans continued to sell pipeline equipment, the United States agreed not to attempt to enforce the import bans or other penalties, and both sides agreed to study the issue of East–West trade.

The pipeline crisis settled nothing, and no one west of the Berlin wall should be satisfied with the outcome. It revealed the basic disagreement between the United States and its allies regarding the value of East–West trade. In all of the hyperbole about the U.S. trade sanctions and their effect on the West Europeans, the United States was distracted from its real intention — to convince the Soviets to lift the burdens of martial law in Poland. Another ambiguous study was conducted that delayed concerted action on the pipeline and made it increasingly likely, as events have proven, that Western Europe would become more dependent on Soviet energy supplies.

In anticipation of the expiration and renewal of the Export Administration Act, the U.S. business community seized upon the pipeline incident to rally its supporters on Capitol Hill. This use of export controls demonstrated, they argued, the foolishness of unilateral decisions not fully supported by NATO. Furthermore, controls could not be enforced abroad on subsidiaries and licensees unless the foreign host government agreed. So any extraterritorial application of U.S. controls was doomed to failure. Some even argued that any use of controls on exports was counterproductive, but this was generally a minority view. The prevailing business view would limit controls to less controversial cases.

Congress could not easily resolve these issues surrounding the Export Administration Act. The hard-liners insist on increased protection and surveillance over exports, citing losses of technology to the bloc. On the other side, the export caucus sought freer trade, particularly within the West. As a result of a deadlock, the act was not renewed before it expired on September 30, 1983, and the president was forced to impose controls by executive order. If he had not done so, there would have been no authority to prevent East bloc sales. Even with the executive order, many legal questions arise about the scope and terms of his authority in the absence of the Congressional legislation.

Finally, in early 1985, the act was renewed with some language protecting existing contracts from arbitrary export controls and giving greater weight to competitive products available overseas that might compete with controlled U.S. products. It is viewed as essentially a renewal of the act's basic provisions. In fact, many argue that a simple extension of the present act for several years is better than either extreme position discussed on Capitol Hill.

DOING BUSINESS WITH THE SOVIETS

An understanding of the Soviet system of trade must begin with the basics. The fundamental principle of Marxism-Leninism in the Soviet Union and its satellites is the ownership by the state of all means of production. Private property is limited to personal belongings and small-scale businesses. Increasingly, the satellites and China are experimenting with other exceptions to allow for small private gardens and farms, small enterprises, and some private merchandising; but these remain very much the exceptions. Still the vast majority of production, all heavy industry, and all international trade are state-owned and controlled.

The Soviet system was enshrined in its 1977 Constitution, but it harks back to a decree signed by Lenin on April 22, 1918. That decree established the state monopoly of foreign trade. All party Congresses since the 1920s have confirmed the monopoly as one of the most important links in the Soviet economic policy. It forms the basis of all trade, economic, scientific, and technical cooperation with foreign countries.

The instrument used is the Soviet Trade Representation system, in existence since the 1920s. All foreign trade must be handled by trade representatives and by foreign trade organizations of the state. The theory is that such concentration increases the buying power of the state and thereby increases economic efficiency. The state would have bargaining power equal to or greater than the largest foreign corporations, trusts, or syndicates.

Buying power is concentrated through the coordination of industry and sector plans. In Gosplan, the State Planning Committee, five-year plans are developed through consultation with the other ministries and government agencies. These plans specify the levels and patterns of foreign trade, the imports from each foreign country, and the Soviet user or consumer. Conversely, production for export is specified by sector and industry. Foreign trade is an integral part of the five-year plan and its annual components.

The end users are factories, state farms, and other organizations. They must submit their requests for imports to Gosplan for incorporation in the plans, often years in advance of actual need. This system obviously inhibits flexibility and responsiveness. Industries cannot readily or easily adjust their production to meet new demand, technology, or fashions; they remain captive of plans made years before.

Once the plan, with its import and export components, is accepted, the Ministry of Foreign Trade implements the trade aspects. The ministry arranges trade agreements with other countries, controls the trade representatives and commercial counselors in foreign countries, conducts market and trade-related research, and actually conducts the buying and selling through the Foreign Trade Organizations (FTOs).

The FTOs form the heart of the Soviet system. They are authorized by the Ministry of Foreign Trade to make purchases abroad, as specified in the import plan. There are more than forty FTOs, each of which handles a range of commodities and products, usually both exporting and importing goods of the same general type. For example, *V/O Exportlyon* exports and imports natural fibers (wool, cotton, flax, etc.), textiles and fabrics; *V/O Tractoroexport* exports and imports tractors, agricultural equipment, and road building machinery. Each FTO is an arm of the Ministry of Foreign Trade and has the exclusive right to trade its products with other countries, regardless of whether the foreign entity is a private corporation or a state agency. Thus trade with the Soviet Union involves at least one government, the USSR, in all details of the transaction.

In carrying out their responsibilities, the FTOs work closely with the end-user organizations. The end-users will specify their requirements and their budgets for imports. They will set the specifications of products to be exported. However, the FTOs, as autonomous organizations, decide with whom to trade and under what terms and conditions. They charge commissions for their services and in many ways act like private commercial traders, particularly when dealing with the industrialized West. In 1977 the U.S. Department of Commerce estimated that many of the FTOs had turnovers exceeding $1 billion a year, ranking among the largest international traders in the world.

Though they may act like commercial organizations, they carry out their transactions according to the overall foreign policy of the USSR. As the U.S. Commerce Department report states,

> Political and economic considerations at a higher level, however, can also play a decisive role in determining ultimate purchasing decisions. The U.S.S.R. may conclude contracts with foreign firms in support of particular foreign policy objectives or for financial reasons, such as credit availability and terms beneficial to the economy as a whole (U.S. Department of Commerce 1983a: 16).

This means that no deals may be made without state approval; every transaction must conform to state policy as well as make trade or commercial sense. This point is so basic to East–West trade that it cannot be overstressed.

Once a deal is concluded, the mechanics of distribution and merchandising are strictly controlled by the state. Financing and payment is handled by the state Bank for Foreign Trade—another monopoly delegated to a state organization. Advertising of foreign products in the Soviet Union also is strictly controlled, and must be handled through *V/O Vneshtorgreklama*, another FTO. Any exhibitions of products within the USSR must be held in conjunction with the FTOs, the USSR Chamber of Commerce and Industry, or local governments; a free consumer market does not exist.

Even commercial representation is tightly controlled, with offices of U.S. firms allowed only if they conform to the terms of an agreement between the United States and the USSR. For example, no more than five foreigners are allowed to work for any foreign company. Explicit customs regulations apply to imports such as samples, office supplies, and office equipment. Even with the impetus to U.S. trade during the years of detente, no more than thirty companies established such representative offices. The U.S. Commerce Department warned that doing business in the Soviet Union is only for those who persevere—substantial costs are involved, and it might take one to three years to negotiate the first contract.

VARIATIONS ON THE SOVIET THEME

As the first country to become a communist state, Russia established the precedents in trade policy and politics. However, as other countries have adopted or have been forced to adopt the instruments of the communist state, differences in approach have surfaced. Not all members of the Council on Mutual Economic Assistance (CMEA), to give the bloc its proper name, manage their economies in the same ways. Mongolia, Cuba and Vietnam have quite different needs and solutions from Poland, East Germany, and Hungary, for example. Even greater differences appear in the non-CMEA communist states, such as China, and the African states professing communism.

When Eastern Europe fell to the Soviets after World War II, many of the officials installed in the satellite governments were agents of the Soviet Union or schooled in Soviet policies and organizational techniques. They established governments that closely resembled Moscow's. Of course the military presence of the Russian Army keeps the bloc together, but the Soviets also subsidize the other members through below-world market prices for their exports of crude oil and other raw materials, and through outright grants.

In spite of the strong ties binding the CMEA states to the Soviet Union, with time, national character and preferences have begun to assert themselves. This occurred dramatically in Yugoslavia in the 1950s and Hungary in the 1956 uprising, and almost as dramatically in Czechoslovakia in 1968 and Poland in 1981. All of these countries wanted to extricate themselves from the Soviets and their inflexible systems. Unable to do so politically, they have begun to experiment with varieties of state ownership that allow for more growth and freedom in the economy.

The Yugoslavs have gone furthest, separating themselves in the 1950s from the coordination of East bloc plans by CMEA. Although the state still owns all means of production, each enterprise is managed by its employees and controls its own pricing and production. There is competition between enterprises as well as from imports. There is no state monopoly of foreign trade in the Soviet sense; each enterprise manages its own trade, subject to the strict foreign exchange controls through which the six Yugoslavian republics regulate imports and exports.

In fact, Western investors establishing joint ventures in Yugoslavia express great concern about the shortage of foreign exchange and the limitations it places on importing needed raw materials and repatriating profits. Nevertheless, Yugoslavia has proved hospitable to numerous foreign investors who find ways of dealing with the complexities and rigidities of the worker-management system.

Western investors and traders have had less success penetrating the rest of Eastern Europe. In spite of changes in the basis for external trade, most East European countries remain closed and highly regulated economies. Hungary and Romania have gone further than most to instill a degree of openness, but the state organs remain paramount. Poland and Hungary have reformed their trade by allowing the larger enterprises to handle their own trade, bypassing the FTO middlemen. The other countries have allowed producers to set up their own FTOs or to integrate them into the producing organization. Only the Soviet Union retains the classical Leninist system.

Part of the explanation for the lack of change in the Soviet system is its relative insularity. Ninety-five percent of Soviet production stays at home; of the portion exported, half goes to the controlled CMEA members. In contrast to the managers and officials of the East Europeans, the Soviet managers have little contact with the West, with Western management, or with the capitalist economies. They have little need to improve quality or reliability for competition in Western markets, and few incentives to improve efficiency or productivity. As long as they remain insulated, the productivity of the civilian Soviet economy will lag behind the East Europeans and far behind the West.

The Soviets have concluded long-term trade agreements with most of the Western European nations. A program of cooperation with staunchly capitalist West Germany has been in place for twenty-five years. In fact, West Germany has become one of the defenders of

East–West trade, with German industry supplying a higher proportion of Soviet imports than any other European country. In a recent announcement, the Bonn government stated it could not accept tighter restrictions on U.S. technology resales through German firms. Germany may even pass legislation, already passed in the United Kingdom and France, prohibiting local firms from carrying out U.S. licensing controls (Bangemann 1984: 178).

All of these intergovernmental agreements between the USSR and its trading partners establish joint commissions between the governments to monitor trade on a continuing basis. Some agreements go further and actually specify contracts to be signed. For example, a recent agreement with France, signed in early 1984, specified some $1 billion worth of industrial equipment to be purchased by the USSR from France—five times the 1983 purchases. In return, France agreed to buy $1.2 billion worth of natural gas above and beyond the amounts already contracted for. Chemical and agricultural purchases were also covered in the agreement.

Similar agreements exist between the USSR and the developing countries. In some cases the agreements are not as specific, but merely state objectives for increasing trade. The 1980 India–USSR agreement, for instance, states a goal of increasing trade by 50 to 100 percent by 1986, with continued growth to 1990. Of the 101 developing countries trading with the USSR, 79 do so under such bilateral agreements. In all, the USSR has 116 such agreements around the world.

Just as the USSR uses bilateral agreements and commissions, so too do the East bloc Europeans. The U.S. Commerce Department led several of these joint commissions with the Hungarians, the Romanians, and the Yugoslavs. A new joint commission on commerce and trade was established with China in 1982 to provide a forum for resolving trade problems. Secretary Baldrige revived the U.S.–USSR joint commission, traveling to Moscow in 1984 for the first meeting in seven years. In every case the prime topic of discussion is the same: How can trade be facilitated and promoted? China, Hungary, and Romania are also concerned about the annual renewal by the United States of their most-favored nation status. But as long as they do not interfere with the rights of religious minorities or Jewish emigration, the administration and the Congress will continue to support MFN status.

THE CHINESE EXPERIMENT

China has attempted to avoid the rigidities of the Soviet system. It is now experimenting with new incentive plans that look quite Western in comparison with its previous practices or with the East bloc. China allows joint ventures with the same limitations on ownership as in the bloc, but with local enterprise decisionmaking. China has even established foreign trade zones, in which foreign companies may set up shop free from the restrictions placed on them elsewhere in the country. The gradual assimilation of Hong Kong, starting in 1997, will create the biggest "special economic zone" since a great deal of autonomy will be given to Hong Kong to run its commercial life as before, subject to Chinese sovereignty.

The control of trade in China has been successively centralized, decentralized, and recentralized in the 1970s and early 1980s. After the chaotic years of the Great Leap Forward and the rule of the Red Guards, gaining control of external trade relations seemed paramount. The first contacts with the United States and the first visit by President Nixon provided impetus. Later, after agreements regulating trade between the United States and China were signed, some relaxation occurred in the control of imports and exports delegated to provinces, large cities, and large enterprises. This heralded the beginning of a "China boom."

Many foreign companies rushed into China in the late 1970s with visions of large contracts and quick profits, only to be disappointed when China itself realized the limits of its capacity to develop. Projects have been abandoned, deals renounced, and Western businesses now have adjusted to more realistic expectations. China remains interested in acquiring Western technology and industry, but on its own terms and in its own time. It prefers to do business with foreign governments under bilateral agreements, rather than with private firms. As a result China has concluded a number of such agreements with the United States for energy development, transportation planning, banking, tourism, and most recently, telecommunications research and development. This last agreement may not be approved by Congress, however, given the opposition of the U.S. Department of Defense to the transfer of sensitive technologies, such as fiber-optics transmission of communications.

As the Chinese deputy minister of foreign trade explained in 1982, in order to avoid the problems of the past, there has been a certain amount of recentralization of control over trade decisions. Authorization to import, previously granted at lower levels, must now be secured from the Ministry of Foreign Trade in Beijing. As a result of this policy, China has kept its imports to the levels of its exports and managed to avoid incurring either trade deficits or debts to foreign creditors.

In all of these centrally planned, nonmarket economies, the state plays a role well beyond that played in the market economies. Even where the state's hand is not seen, it is felt. To understand more about the state role, we next turn to the question of how these countries fit into the GATT system and how they conduct their trade relations with the market economy states.

NONMARKET ECONOMIES IN THE INTERNATIONAL SYSTEM

The central problem of East–West trade relations is the incompatibility of the central planning system with the assumptions of the GATT. The GATT assumes that imports and exports are guided by commercial considerations. Private firms, stimulated by the profit motive and making decisions according to relative prices, handle trade transactions. These decisions are affected by tariffs, which raise or lower prices. Nontariff barriers and other obstacles to trade should therefore be eliminated. Each trading nation should grant the same treatment that it grants one trading partner to all others, following the principle of most-favored nation treatment.

Every one of these assumptions is missing in the centrally planned countries. First, imports and exports are not guided by commercial considerations but by a host of political, military, diplomatic, and domestic economic considerations. Trade does not flow of its own accord but according to plan.

Second, private firms do not exist in centrally planned economies, and trade is handled exclusively by organs of the state; there are few independent decisionmakers. These organizations do not attempt to maximize profits, and very few have any control over the prices they charge.

Third, the most serious incompatibility is the failure of centrally planned countries to take account of relative prices. This means the principle of comparative advantage cannot be applied because products are not bought from the cheapest sources. Nonmarket countries do not know the costs of the products they buy and sell, which causes grave problems for Western governments attempting to detect and prove dumping.

Fourth, since imports are planned based on the difference between expected production and expected consumption, tariffs have little or no effect on the buying decisions of central planners. Further, the tariff schedule of a centrally planned economy is as much a fiction as its prices.

Fifth, central planning itself is the greatest nontariff barrier and cannot be eliminated in a nonmarket country. The state, through the plan, determines whether a domestic or a foreign product will be bought. This is the starkest kind of government barrier to imports.

Sixth, bloc currencies are not freely convertible on the market and their relative uselessness outside the countries of issue requires trade to be balanced through countertrade and through other devices described in more detail in the next chapter. This limits the types of transactions that can be conducted.

Lastly, because of centralized planning, subsidies, coordination in production, and favorable pricing between CMEA governments, there is clearly discrimination violating the MFN principle.

Given all of these problems, it is not surprising that the East bloc countries, China, and the other centrally planned countries cannot participate fully in the GATT or in the international trading system. When it began its movement away from central planning, delegated pricing, and production decisions to worker-managed enterprises, Yugoslavia was able to fit into the GATT. It joined as a full member in 1966.

Poland joined the following year, but under quite different circumstances. Poland had participated in the Kennedy Round of tariff negotiations, indicating its interest in GATT membership. In order to overcome some of the problems cited above, Poland pledged to increase its imports from all of the GATT members by seven percent per year. Its performance on this pledge was to be reviewed each year. If Poland failed to reach this goal, GATT members could withdraw trade concessions they had granted to Poland (Dam 1970: 237).

Although Poland has not achieved this goal in recent years, the major Western powers were willing to overlook its shortcoming as long as progress was being made. The United States used this failure as justification for withdrawing MFN treatment for Poland in 1982, after realizing that the 1981 sanctions had not affected martial law. Even when playing power politics, trade lawyers look for legal bases for their actions.

The status of other East bloc countries varies. Czechoslovakia was a member of the GATT before it became communist, so its membership survives in a nonmarket limbo. Hungary has moved in the direction of decentralizing pricing and production decisions and has been welcomed into the GATT as a constructive member. Romania remains an interested observer, taking part in discussion, but not in GATT decisions. East Germany, Bulgaria, Cuba, Vietnam, and Mongolia — the other CMEA members — do not participate.

The status of China in the GATT will raise these problems anew as China applies for membership. Many developed countries fear the manufacturing potential of China can surpass them in textile and other low-value products that are currently causing problems. Discrimination against Chinese products, therefore, is now legitimate, without the necessity of proving difficult antidumping cases. On the other hand, the billion-person Chinese market continues to lure the Western business. Without a stable trade relationship, business suffers and is totally at the discretion of Chinese bureaucrats. Is there more to lose or to gain by admitting China to full GATT membership?

Given the ambiguous situation of the CMEA and other nonmarket countries under the GATT, it has not proven a satisfactory framework for reintegrating those countries into the world trading system. East–West trade has suffered as a result. Taking the place of the GATT and general trading rules has been a series of bilateral arrangements between East and West detailing what will be bought, sold, and how.

UPS AND DOWNS OF EAST–WEST TRADE

East–West trade rests on the shifting foundations of political relations between the superpowers. The modern era of those relations began with the Nixon administration and detente. In 1972 two-way trade between the United States and the USSR was only $100 million, a minuscule amount for such large countries. At the Moscow Summit Meeting on May 28, 1972, President Nixon and Chairman Brezhnev signed an agreement establishing a basis for relations between the United States and the USSR. The two countries agreed to regard trade and economic ties as "...an important and indispensable element of strengthening their bilateral relations...", jointly undertaking to promote the growth of such ties (U.S. Department of Commerce 1983a). Following the summit the countries drafted a series of trade arrangements, including a maritime agreement, the settlement of outstanding lendlease claims, and a trade agreement.

The trade agreement, concluded in October 1972, has never taken effect. In part, it sets down guidelines to facilitate trade, including the granting of most-favored nation treatment to the USSR. Legislation authorizing this MFN status was included in the 1974 Trade Act, but with an important proviso. Under the Jackson–Vanik amendment, MFN could be granted only if the USSR gave assurances about the emigration of Jews from the Soviet Union and the treatment of religious minorities and dissidents. The USSR viewed these conditions as intolerable, and the trade agreement could not take effect.

Its terms, although not effective or binding in a legal sense, nevertheless form the framework for U.S.-USSR trade. They provide for the use of convertible currency, third-party arbitration of disputes, establishment of trade offices in Moscow and Washington, availability of business facilities, and general trade promotion. A joint U.S.-USSR Commercial Commission was established to monitor trade relations between the two countries. Later agreements added provisions for more business promotion activities.

All of these arrangements are now in limbo. The budding trade relationship suffered first the shock of Afghanistan, then the Polish crisis. Trade between the United States and the USSR reached its all-time high of almost $4 billion in 1979, forty times the amount just seven years before. As a result of the Afghanistan invasion in December of 1979, the United States boycotted the Moscow Olympics, embargoed grain sales, and cracked down on oil and gas technology sales to the USSR. Trade in 1980 dropped to half that of 1979. The election of President Reagan signaled the end of detente and the beginning of a colder relationship with the Soviet Union. The military takeover in Poland provided the catalyst for the final steps in reversing the gains in East-West trade of the previous decade. New controls were placed on trade, direct airflights were cancelled, fishing rights were terminated, and the pipeline crisis was triggered.

In spite of these ups and downs, certain U.S. companies have been able to maintain their presence and their connections with the Soviets. The most notable is Armand Hammer's Occidental Petroleum Company and its twenty-year, $20 billion contract signed in 1973 to supply ammonia fertilizer plants and to buy part of its production. Other companies like Pepsi Cola have continued to export and import throughout the periods of tension. The Soviet Union has also proved to be one of the best customers for U.S. wheat and other agricultural products since their own system consistently fails to feed the population. As some of the U.S. companies doing business there like to point out, the Soviet Union is one of the few countries with which the United States enjoys a trade surplus.

The lessons to be learned from East–West trade can be summarized. First, no trade takes place legally in strategic goods or technology, although evidence is mounting about the quantity of illegal exports reaching the Soviet Union. A large potential volume of trade is simply off limits.

Second, the structure of the Soviet Union and the other nonmarket economies limits any trade that does occur to state trading. Trade monopolies are inherent in the communist states, although the conduct of these monopolies is handled differently in different countries. Because of this structure, the principles and assumptions of the GATT are basically incompatible with the nonmarket countries. Whether they will ever be able to evolve into full-fledged members of the GATT trading community is an open question.

Lastly, all trade with the centrally planned countries is subject to political, not market, imperatives. East–West trade tracks political relations very closely. The centrally planned countries use bilateral agreements and commissions to attempt to overcome these problems, spelling out the rules of the game bilaterally. In so doing, however, they introduce new complexities and rigidities into the trading system, adding even more to the burden of trade managed by governments.

12 BALANCED TRADE

It is increasingly common for countries, regardless of their levels of development or their political systems, to attempt to manage their trade through barter, countertrade, and similar techniques. These operations can take many forms, some quite complicated and involved. Sometimes the complications are necessary, other times they disguise the true nature of the transaction. Sometimes barter is mandated by the state, other times it is convenient for the traders to act as if it were. Most observers of the trade field believe that countertrade and its variations will only increase in importance in the future. As one business magazine opined, "The newest threat to open, multilateral world trade is coming from the oldest form of trade. Governments are replacing money and credit as the medium of international exchange with a plague of variations on barter" (*Business Week* 1982).

Several different types of transactions fall under the general heading of countertrade. Some of the most common forms now seen in international trade are:

* Barter—the exchange of goods or services between two trading partners without resorting to money. If no currency changes hands, then the values of the goods or services are defined as equal.

149

- Counterpurchase arrangement — an agreement linking exports and imports of unrelated products, whether bartered or not. Also known as offset sales, parallel purchases, or reciprocal purchases.
- Coproduction arrangement — an agreement linking exports and imports of related products, such as intermediate component imports to make finished product exports. Also known as import compensation.
- Clearing arrangement — an agreement between governments to trade with the objective of keeping a balance over time of exports and imports. A clearing arrangement essentially institutes barter at the macroeconomic level between countries.
- Compensation arrangement — an agreement between an exporter of a plant or factory and its purchaser by which the exporter agrees to take back product from the plant as part of the price.

Complications abound in working out these different types of arrangements. For example, products to be delivered in the future must be valued in the present. Future exchange rate fluctuations must be taken into account through formulas and adjustments. If the party taking back compensation product cannot sell the product through its own channels, it may turn over the product to a third party, usually at a discount. Intermediaries, called *switch houses*, and countertrade specialists have sprung up to handle these unwanted products. The products may even be diverted to third countries by these practices. And if a government finances the original export, it may also be a party to the transaction.

U.S. opposition to government-imposed barter and countertrade stems from several sources. Countertrade limits the operation of the free market. It increases the role of government in trade management and leads to bilateral trade deals, rather than to an open multilateral system. Dumping can be disguised and import controls can be evaded. Since imports into a countertrading country are allowed only if there is a compensating export commitment, the result, in effect, is indirect import licensing, in violation of the GATT.

The extent of countertrade is hard to measure. The only reliable statistics available are found in East–West trade, and even that documentation is incomplete. Based on those data, the OECD estimates that countertrade now amounts to 15 to 20 percent of all East–West trade, a very conservative estimate. The official U.S. Department of

Commerce estimate for several years has been that about 20 percent of all trade, West–West as well as East–West, is countertrade. In March 1984 a Department of Commerce specialist was quoted as saying that the current amount of countertrade ranges from 20 to 30 percent, and that it is expected to reach 50 percent by the end of the century. Eighty-eight countries now request or require barter, up from twenty-eight, three years ago (Walsh 1984). Clearly this situation bears examination.

Barter assuredly is not a new practice—most primitive societies have employed it in the absence of reliable currencies. When governments became involved in barter, it was given the more elaborate name of *compensation agreements*. In the 1930s Germany developed the first modern examples of barter and clearing agreements because of the problems of its currency and its foreign exchange controls. The first agreement was signed with Hungary in 1932, and by 1937 Germany had negotiated agreements with every European country, except Britain, and with several Latin American countries. These clearing arrangements required a bilateral balance of accounts on an annual basis, covering not only trade but all financial flows. Germany thereby had access to both markets and raw materials that otherwise would not have been available to it (Kenwood and Lougheed 1983: 213).

COUNTERTRADE IN NONMARKET COUNTRIES

A discussion of countertrade should start with those who practice it most assiduously, the nonmarket countries of the communist world. Given their central planning, inconvertible currencies, and monopolies of foreign trade, the communist countries quickly developed countertrade techniques. Nonmarket countries actively manage their external trade by attempting to balance imports and exports to avoid deficits, and thus debts in hard currencies.

Countertrade plays a major role in keeping accounts balanced, but this is not the only reason for the practice. Perhaps the most important influence on the growth of countertrade was the managerial and marketing weakness of the centrally planned economies. Countertrade puts the onus on the foreign party to find markets for the countertraded goods.

For example, if McDonnell Douglas takes hams in part payment for selling aircraft to Poland, then McDonnell Douglas and not Polish enterprises must find markets outside Poland for the hams. The Polish government has shifted the burden of marketing from the Polish packers, who probably would not do a good job, to the foreign partner who must do a good job in order to realize any profit on the transaction. The state trading monopoly and the relatively few FTOs handling trade make such marketing shifts possible.

Another complication is pricing. DC-8s are not normally sold for other products, so McDonnell Douglas does not set prices in so many pounds of canned ham. The negotiations may start with a dollar figure, but after successive rounds have added, subtracted, and converted aircraft to meat, the stated "shadow" dollar price has little, if any, meaning. This presents both problems and opportunities.

At earlier stages of the development of countertrade, Western traders regarded barter as a last resort, a method by which the unproductive East could dispose of products they could not otherwise sell. The merchandise was shoddy, the practice was questionable, and technologies were not developed. If the product from the West was desirable enough, the Eastern bloc countries would allocate scarce foreign exchange for its purchase. And what Western business would like to admit that its product was not in demand? Countertrade lived in the shadows, and few admitted to its existence.

As a result, a cottage industry of countertrade specialists arose in Europe, primarily in Vienna, which considered itself the crossroads of East–West trade. These specialists knew the products of the East, and more important, how to get rid of them. They would take the products at a substantial discount and dispose of them for the Western exporter. Thus a Western business could calculate in advance just how much it would "lose" from the disposal of the Eastern products. The business then would increase the price of the products sold to the East in order to cover the loss. Everyone was happy: the Western business made a sale with an expected profit on its own products; the Eastern bloc FTO gained both an import from the West and an export to the West; and the countertrade specialist acquired goods at a discount, for resale outside the bloc.

The problem with such transactions surfaces when an East bloc product appears on a Western market. A Western producer may be concerned about the pricing of the import from the East, and may file an antidumping suit. The Western producer would allege that the sale was occurring below fair-market value (i.e., the product was being dumped). It is difficult enough to determine the true costs of production and pricing of nonmarket economy products; and this is compounded by the arbitrariness of the price established by the countertrade sale. It is understandable that government officials dealing with dumping cases dislike countertrade, whereas some international traders have embraced it.

A few examples will give the flavor of this trade. The Soviet Union is buying much-needed construction equipment from Komatsu and Mitsubishi in Japan, some of which is being used on the Siberian gas pipeline construction. The USSR is paying for the equipment with Siberian timber. In another deal, Yugoslavia requires the Italian automaker Fiat to buy Yugoslav goods equal in value to the parts and components shipped into Yugoslavia. Fiat buys automobiles from its Yugoslav licensee. In a buyback arrangement, China requires another Italian company, Technotrade, to take coal for sale abroad as part of the price of a $500 million contract to expand and modernize its mining industry (*Business Week* 1982).

Japanese and European companies have long adapted to the needs of countertrade in order to do business in the East. U.S. companies held out, insisting on cash. Today, many U.S. executives are learning that countertrade may be necessary when dealing with cash-poor, foreign-exchange-limited countries. Trading companies have dealt with countertrade for years, and now new trading companies are being set up in the United States to handle these countertrade obligations. Even major companies have established departments to find markets for products they do not make or ordinarily sell. Some have found that barter can also be profitable.

Nonmarket countries of the East bloc resort to countertrade to:

- preserve scarce foreign exchange
- shift the marketing burden
- force "extra sales" in the West
- disguise dumping
- use Western distribution channels, and
- gain access to Western marketing technology without "paying" for it

Many of the developing countries of the "South" face the same problems and have turned to countertrade to solve them.

THIRD WORLD COUNTERTRADE

Development economists are greatly tempted to interfere with markets. The balance of payments of most developing countries is of continuing concern; their imports perennially exceed their exports. In the drive to develop industry and commerce in poorer countries, planners and government officials alike see merit in an export-driven development plan. This view is reinforced by the World Bank, which lends money at low-interest rates for development projects. The Bank encourages import-substituting industries as well as export-oriented projects for which markets must be found.

The International Monetary Fund usually prescribes the reduction of imports and the increase of exports in its plans for ailing debtor nations and will not provide temporary financing unless the debtor agrees to this action. Lastly, the business communities of developing countries see exports as the way to break out of limited local markets.

All of these forces put pressure on developing countries to promote exports. A large steel mill built and owned by the government with low-interest loans cannot be left idle; it must produce to provide the jobs for which it was planned. If the domestic market cannot absorb the products, then they must be exported. Why not impose a countertrade obligation on importers to take the product? Surplus commodities, surplus production, raw materials, semifinished products, consumer goods: all can be countertraded.

If the deal is big enough or the government of a developing country is involved, then countertrade becomes a viable option. For example, Iran traded its oil for $200 million worth of frozen meat from New Zealand; the deal was made between Iran's nationalized oil industry and New Zealand's quasi-governmental Meat Board. Brazil's government extracted commitments from automakers to export $21 billion in cars and other products through 1989 in return for the right to import duty-free parts for Brazilian plants. Brazil also required Hughes Aircraft and Canada's Spar Aerospace to buy $130 million in Brazilian products before it agreed to allow the two countries to sell a space satellite to the government (*Business Week* 1982). In all of these cases the government was one of the trading partners and also imposed countertrade requirements.

Even where the government is not part of the transaction, it may impose barter to help the economy. In many cases countertrade is used to introduce products into otherwise closed markets. It may also be used to help dispose of products in soft markets. A well-publicized example of this was Jamaica's requirement that General Motors finance its sales of trucks to Jamaica by arranging for the sale of Jamaica's alumina in a down market. This shifted some of the loss, and risk of further loss, to GM. The irony of this situation is that it was imposed by the free-market government of President Seaga, not his socialist predecessor. A further irony is that the arrangement was materially aided by the U.S. Embassy's commercial section, in spite of the Reagan administration's sustained opposition to barter arrangements imposed by governments.

Another interesting case is Indonesia. That country suffered declining markets for several of its major export products. Failure to export not only would have foreign exchange consequences but also would reflect badly on Indonesian government planning and support for the export industries. As a result Indonesia introduced a "temporary" countertrade plan, which requires any foreign bidder on government or state-sector contracts of more than $750,000 to buy for export an equal amount from a list of approximately thirty specified Indonesian products. The United States objected strenuously to this requirement, as did several European governments. As Secretary of State Shultz stressed to Indonesian officials, there is no substitute for money in international trade. In the end, however, Japanese, German, and other companies began to do business under these rules and U.S. companies had to comply.

The most extreme development in countertrade occurs in the bilateral clearing arrangements between two countries. Under these arrangements trade is not only monitored but also controlled to keep it within predetermined limits. This type of agreement allows trade between convertible and nonconvertible currency countries and provides protection to both. The agreement between Brazil and East Germany, for example, has an annual review of trade. If the imbalance between the countries becomes too great, then trading stops.

Clearing arrangements rigidify the system and directly involve government in managing trade. The USSR had thirty clearing arrangements in 1979. Even market countries like Brazil, with seventeen such agreements, and Mexico with nineteen, have found them useful. The developed countries of Europe, Japan, and the United States have so far resisted the temptation, but the pressures may dictate similar solutions. Meanwhile, a growing portion of East–South trade is becoming bilateralized in this way.

As long as there are hard currency crunches in the world, countries will need to find new ways to promote their exports. Even with debt rescheduling and easing of debt repayment terms, developing countries will continue to face foreign exchange shortages in paying for needed imports. There will be severe pressures for these countries to adopt countertrade. Barter will grow in importance, unless the industrialized countries unify against it, open their markets even wider, or lighten the debt burden to the point of irrelevance. None of these three possibilities seems likely.

THE MILITARY TRADE MANAGERS

Another major way governments become involved in barter is through trade in defense and military equipment. Countries without central planning and without foreign exchange problems may still employ countertrade to support their military procurement.

Weapons trade raises sensitive issues in most countries. No one likes to be called a "merchant of death." Nevertheless most countries have armaments industries and most support efforts to promote those industries in export markets. These industries range from relatively small, specialized industries — such as Chile's manufacture and export of scatter bombs — to the highly diverse and sophisticated industries of France, the United Kingdom, and the United States. In fact, these three industrialized countries account for a very large proportion of free-world arms sales.

Governments participate heavily in this trade. Through bilateral agreements, the United States supplies military equipment to foreign governments. It lends money on easy terms to finance the purchase of U.S.-made military hardware; it sells obsolete equipment to friendly governments at bargain prices; and it provides training and support to foreign armies, navies and air forces, indirectly pushing U.S. products. It backs U.S. aircraft, weapons, and other suppliers against foreign competition whenever a foreign government is in the market. The U.S. government, like most others, is directly involved in this trade.

The United States has also pushed for interchangeability within NATO so that the military forces use as much similar equipment as possible. Obviously this drive confronts national preferences in Europe to purchase from European sources. The United States itself is prevented from buying from foreign sources unless certain stringent conditions are met: the quality of the foreign product must be equal or superior to the domestic, and its price at least 15 percent lower. Where competition is open, however, as in major fighter procurement in countries not producing aircraft, the negotiations often hinge on how much coproduction or offset the foreign manufacturer is offering.

Coproduction means that the foreign supplier is willing to subcontract part of the manufacture or assembly to local companies. When NATO was purchasing a new fighter in the mid 1970s, the competition was between the French Mirage, made by Dassault, and the U.S. F-16, made by Northrup. The technical evaluations were not decisive in determining the winner, and it came down to which company would subcontract more work in the purchasing countries, Norway and the Netherlands. Northrup won with a net of some 30 percent of the work to be performed in various European locations.

Offset means the foreign supplier agrees to purchase goods to offset a percentage of his sale. These purchases are another way of balancing the trade effects. For example, General Electric agreed to buy Swedish products to offset the contract awarded GE to supply engines for the Swedish JAS fighter. In another deal, Canada is buying McDonnell Douglas F-18 fighter aircraft worth $2.4 billion, but in return the company will help find markets for $2.9 billion worth of Canadian products.

The newest country to impose similar requirements is Saudi Arabia, which in 1984 said it will require from suppliers of military equipment that at least 35 percent of the contract value be made in local investment in Saudi Arabia. The first large contract under this new rule was the Peaceshield support system for the airborne warning and control system (AWACS), won by Boeing and a group of contractors. The must now put together a package of manufacturing investments attractive to the Saudi government.

Coproduction and offset arrangements are not limited to the military but can extend to the whole range of government procurement. In buying aircraft, foreign governments look for as much local assembly, outfitting, and components as possible when considering rival bids. With the increased competition since 1975 between the U.S. aircraft manufacturers and the European Airbus, foreign governments have been able to impose such requirements in an increasing number of cases. In fact all major foreign government power, construction, building, and hospital projects may now depend on offset arrangements.

In the face of these developments, U.S. companies have had to adjust their position on countertrade and offset. U.S. firms are noted for their ability to adapt to changing circumstances. They will do whatever is necessary to secure a deal. If barter and offset are the new rules, they will adapt. Moreover, they look at the profit potential on both ends of the transaction. Instead of treating the countertrade obligation as a problem, they see an opportunity to make money. Some have even set up separate profit centers to maximize the opportunity.

A number of major U.S. companies have taken this approach. Some have set up countertrade departments to handle the bartered goods. Others have relaxed long-standing objections and agreed to barter rather than insist on cash. A few have even set up export trading companies to use their expertise to handle countertrade products and obligations for other companies. Under the terms of the Export Trading Company Act of 1982, commercial banks can own export trading companies (ETCs). Most of the approximately twenty-five banks with ETCs have stated that handling countertrade was one of the prime reasons for setting them up. There is even a loose association of countertrade professionals of major U.S. multinationals; a sure sign that countertrade has arrived.

How will the U.S. government react to these trends? First, it is extremely unlikely that the United States itself will ever impose countertrade obligations. The U.S. belief in the free market transcends any particular president, administration, or party. The United States is too committed to the GATT and the multilateral system to seek clearing arrangements or bilateral agreements limiting trade.

However, U.S. opposition has lessened as countertrade has become more widespread. The United States now distinguishes between countertrade imposed by governments and that arranged willingly by the parties, opposing the former while casting a benign eye on the latter. The United States even helps to arrange countertrade deals through the commercial services in its embassies abroad. As a major arms supplier, the United States must continue to find ways to live with the requirements of foreign countries, especially its allies, that legitimately want a bigger share of the arms procurement trade.

Countertrade and offset are here to stay. They will not be stemmed by action of the United States or other developed countries. Japanese trading companies have a great stake in both ends of trade, importing as much as they export; they will handle countertrade with ease. West Europeans see countertrade as an integral part of their ties to East Europe and the wave of the future in the Third World. Finally, U.S. policy will be determined largely by the objections and complaints of its business community. U.S. business is rapidly adjusting to countertrade and will soon make it as profitable as possible. There are no countervailing forces to the continued expansion of countertrade.

IV LOOKING AHEAD

13 DEALING WITH COMPETITION BETWEEN NATIONS

In our review of the major turning points in the development of international trade, we saw that government intervention in trade matters was for centuries the rule rather than the exception. Kings and barons controlled commerce throughout their lands. Cities and their guilds of artisans and traders wrested part of this control for themselves, jealously guarding their liberties. Their notion of free trade meant freedom from the strictures of the feudal system; it was nothing like the Adam Smith ideal.

Trade began to be associated with national aspirations and prestige only after nation states were firmly developed following the Middle Ages. The premier European trading states — first Venice, then Spain and Portugal, and finally the Netherlands and Britain — associated their wealth and power with their farflung trading relationships. In contrast, the landlocked, the inward-looking, and the balkanized states never developed their trade to the same extent. Britain alone could urge the policies of free trade and enforce them.

The modern trade competition between nations began in earnest during the nineteenth century. The new players on the world stage, first the united colonies of North America, and the united German states challenged the traditional powers. Later Russia, (even before the revolution) and Japan saw trade as the vehicle for their own development. The rush for colonies in Africa and Asia, the jockeying for position in China and Latin America, and the investments in navies were all motivated by this new competition. The twentieth century dawned with the competition in full swing.

The First World War settled new boundaries but not old scores. Interwar trade continued the conflict by other means, with each power eyeing the war preparations of its neighbors, competing for markets and, most importantly, competing for resources. The depression highlighted the vulnerability of the international trade system to political (Smoot–Hawley) and financial (Creditanstalt) shocks. The reliance on the benign leadership of the United Kingdom before 1914 and of the United States after 1918 was not enough. The post–World War II statesmen of Bretton Woods, the United Nations, the Marshall Plan and the Atlantic Alliance created the infrastructure of stability that still exists today. Unfortunately for the development of the international economy in recent years, the benign laissez-faire world envisioned by these leaders has not been achieved. Commercial relations between states have been governed by a solution never intended to serve as the cornerstone. The GATT was intended as only the first implementing agreement of the International Trade Organization. Instead it has had to fill in as the blueprint for the entire system.

PROBLEMS TO BE ADDRESSED

Gaps in the GATT and problems with the international trading system become apparent when confronting the challenges of managed trade as practiced by nations today.

- There are few provisions dealing with the nonmarket economies under which half the world's population lives.
- There are no provisions or rules for state trading practiced by the public sectors of countries.
- There has been only one case brought to the GATT dealing with the impairment of trade agreements by nontariff barriers — surely one of today's most pressing trade problems.
- The GATT does not deal with services, international investment, or other invisibles trade, the fastest growing segment of international activity.
- Disputes brought to the GATT take years to resolve and its decisions cannot be enforced, except by moral suasion.

- The creation of GATT-approved free trade blocs is a patently discriminatory practice, violating its most fundamental principle — most-favored nation treatment.
- Subsidies to encourage trade are not effectively controlled by the GATT, and the OECD agreements are limited in scope.
- The rising expectations of developing countries have led to even more deviations from the general principles of the GATT by according them special and differential treatment.
- The biggest cartel, OPEC, and the other commodity agreements exist wholly outside GATT and any other rules.
- Developing nations uniformly view the GATT as the rich man's club and increasingly favor the United Nations Conference on Trade and Development (UNCTAD).
- The most serious disputes in textiles, steel, autos, and a host of other manufactured products must be settled outside the GATT.

Calls for improving the GATT are fine as far as they go, since an improved GATT can only enhance the overall environment within which trade takes place. But they do not go far enough. As Senator William Roth (Republican of Delaware) recently observed:

> I am afraid that GATT is — much like our own trade appartus — outdated and irrelevant.
> It is clearly time to question the basic premises of GATT — most favored nation trading status for all who seek it regardless of their own practices and special preferences for developing countries. In addition, it is time to "graduate" the newly industrialized countries from special treatment. It makes no sense to treat the Taiwans and Hong Kongs of the world as if they needed the kind of trading advantages given to the Cameroons and Bangladesh.
> If I have anything to say about it, the day of unilateral free trade, courtesy of the United States, is over (Roth 1983).

A broader strategy is necessary, based on a few simple conclusions:

- The United States is and will continue to be both the largest single market and the largest trading nation.
- The United States has not used its market power to the fullest.
- Free trade principles are no longer adhered to by most nations except when it suits their own interests.
- Protection is growing in all countries, regardless of level of development.

- Governments are increasingly involving themselves in international trade for a variety of reasons.

THE U.S. DILEMMA

The United States itself has been a part of the movement toward managing trade. It has allowed the government increasingly to interject itself into the market, with its promotion of the textile agreements, with the orderly marketing agreements for television, steel, footwear, with pressure for the auto agreement, and with the recent decisions on autos, steel, and textiles. U.S. actions have now accumulated to the point where trade management in the U.S. economy is the rule rather than the exception, at least for the most important products. The balance between government action and private action has shifted in the direction of the government. One distinguished observer has succinctly diagnosed the problem:

> The United States remains formally committed to free trade, but it lacks a coherent strategy to deal with protectionist and mercantilistic measures of other nations. Hence, in practice American trade policy is a series of disconnected ad hoc decisions taken largely in response to the specific complaints of politically powerful interests most directly affected. These are by definition usually the least competitive sectors. So long as the impetus behind policy is the desire to reduce the pain, the result can only by accident be the promotion of the common good of either the United States or of the world economy as a whole (Kissinger 1984).

The movement toward managed trade is irreversible. To achieve truly free trade would require dismantling the European Common Market and the East bloc's COMECON; ending the special and differential treatment promoting development in poor countries; removing governments from the airline, communications, trading, insurance, and shipping businesses; eliminating OPEC; outlawing financial and tax incentives for new investment; and most importantly, throwing open protected sectors in all countries to the harsh forces of international competition. Only then would the preconditions be in place for buyers and sellers to make decisions without government interference.

Given the impossibility of this task, the United States must turn its attention away from the elusive goal of universal free trade and focus on what can be done. What changes are possible, given the world as it is, to improve trading relationships between countries, to minimize the adverse effects of managed trade, and to achieve significant advances? It is essential to be very clear about the problems ahead.

First, the United States must recognize that much of the effort other countries put into developing free trade blocs, coordinating their strategies, and building international institutions is aimed at building countervailing forces to U.S. market power. The United States has accepted these actions with a view to building the international economy and the trade system that has served so well.

But the forces ranged against U.S. policies are overwhelming. Countries are increasingly adopting programs to aid their industrial exporters. Moreover, international institutions are being influenced by protectionist ideologies, and by the socialist and nonmarket economy countries, which care little for the liberal international system of free trade. These institutions will bend the rules of trade and investment to suit their new clientele.

Second, as a result of these changes, most countries have lost a world view and now conduct international economic policymaking through excessively self-serving means. They adhere to free trade principles and to the rules of the GATT only when it is in their immediate interest to do so. The poor countries of the South blame the rich North for their problems and rig the rules of trade in an attempt to redress the balance. The backward East takes what it needs from the West without giving fair-market opportunities in return. The OPEC countries manage the trade of the most important commodity in trade — oil — through the world's largest cartel, with the sole objective of maximizing their own earnings. The newly industrializing countries follow in Japan's footsteps to penetrate and exploit the developed country markets wherever possible, without granting access to their own.

Third, protectionism is growing in key sectors and may influence trade generally in the future. In spite of tariff-reduction negotiations among the developed countries, nontariff barriers have not been seriously touched. The tariff reductions themselves have been limited to nonsensitive products and areas. Quotas and high tariffs remain in sensitive areas, even among the most liberal countries. The developed industrialized countries protect their markets whenever and against whomever they can. Protection for infant industries, for new firms, and for government-owned industries is rampant in the Third World. Liberalization is slow, selective, and purchased only at a price.

Fourth, government involvement in trade is growing, further limiting the area within which free trade principles operate. Market decisions are now influenced by, if not directly subject to, intergovernmental agreements in many areas. Complaints of unfair treatment lead to diplomatic protests and new government-to-government "understandings." Subsidies and countersubsidy actions abound. The tendency to protect a domestic market is matched by the exporters desire for certainty, hence the willingness to negotiate orderly marketing agreements, restraint agreements, and all of the other devices for controlling trade. In response to actions brought by domestic producers affected by competition, these "solutions" will only become more common.

Finally, the consensus that existed among the small number of countries meeting in Geneva in 1947 to form the GATT no longer exists. The founders of the GATT had distinct views about its functions and its future but a host of Third World countries now regard the GATT as the rich man's club. Nonmarket countries exist and trade outside the GATT framework. Many members selectively adhere to its principles and its specific sub-agreements or codes, weakening its structure even further. Given the impossibility of rebuilding the consensus today, many of the problems of the international economy cannot and will not be solved by the GATT or the other international institutions.

The United States has benefited from the free trade environment of the postwar period. It is logical to continue to support the principles of free trade and to urge others to do so as well. This must be the long-term objective of U.S. policy.

14 TRADE POLICY FOR THE FUTURE

The implications for the international trading system are not comforting. They lead to policy prescriptions that challenge long-held, fundamental beliefs. They may lead to actions that are difficult to accept but may be necessary to preserve and enhance the U.S. position in a way consistent with the greatest good for the largest number.

The United States should set its sights on goals designed to enlarge, as much as possible, the area within which free trade principles operate. I believe this can be done by judicious use of the principle of reciprocity in trading relationships and by negotiating new free trade areas with those countries that are prepared to do so.

The United States must formulate the new policy principles to:

- develop an effective policy of reciprocity in its trading relationships;
- revise U.S. laws to deal with foreign government targeting, non-market economy exports, foreign subsidies, and dumping so as to diminish criticism that its use of them is protectionist;
- conclude special arrangements with Canada, Mexico, and the Caribbean countries to strengthen the North American economy as a whole;
- strengthen the GATT to deal with the trade issues and disputes arising between governments, not just private traders; and

- form a free trade area with like-minded countries to preserve the largest possible liberal economic environment

STRENGTHENING RECIPROCITY

The free trade system and the GATT are based on the concept of reciprocity. As treated in trade negotiations, reciprocity is defined as "...a broad balance between the reduction in trade barriers offered by the United States and the liberalization secured from the other major trading partners..." (Cline 1983: 122). This has resulted in an exchange of reductions of tariffs and quotas "at the margin," with all products considered together. Thus, while the exchange with any one product or any one country based on actual trade flows may not be equal, the total value of reductions is approximately reciprocal.

Cline has referred to this concept of reciprocity as passive. Once negotiations have established the degree of protection inherent in the levels of tariffs and quotas, no further governmental action is expected or required. Theoretically, there is no further concern for the outcome or results of trade.

The problem with this concept of reciprocity is that it no longer achieves results in the real world. As repeatedly demonstrated in this analysis of trade, tariff levels are only one of many ways in which governments intervene to affect trade flows. In adopting a hands-off approach once tariff negotiations are completed, the United States forgoes the opportunity, *in fact it fails in its duty,* to realize the benefits expected from the negotiation. Tariff protection may have been forfeited with little or nothing gained in return.

This is the problem the new reciprocity movement attempts to address. The new reciprocity would be aggressive rather than passive. It would directly challenge the denial of opportunity in foreign markets and would threaten to withdraw equivalent opportunities in U.S. markets. The principal reciprocity bill before Congress since 1984 was introduced by Senator John Danforth (Republican of Missouri) and has been supported by the Reagan administration. It requires the president to take steps and make legislative proposals to Congress for dealing with unreasonable trade practices of foreign countries that deny fair and equitable market opportunities to U.S. exporters.

In the emerging area of services trade, for example, reciprocity would have immediate impact. The prospect of retaliation for denial of market access could liberalize trade. As Shelp says, ". . .it [retaliation] would probably be a very effective way to erase impediments imposed by one or a limited number of countries" (Shelp 1981: 206). He considers the technique to have particular value for dealing with those outside the established institutions and trading rules, such as the socialist countries that do not participate in the GATT.

In recent years the concept of reciprocity has acquired almost a pejorative meaning. Its critics consider it a code word for protectionism. Several variations of reciprocity have been considered in other legislation, but most would impose a much narrower definition of sectoral, or even bilateral, reciprocity. These bills are properly characterized as protectionist and anti-Japanese in origin. They attempt to deal with symptoms rather than causes. They should not be confused with the broader notion of reciprocity inherent in Senator Danforth's proposal.

What the critics refuse to understand is that a new departure in trade strategy is necessary to deal with government-managed trade. The Danforth proposal would indeed, as Cline warns, ". . .mark the adoption of a new basic trade strategy that would be unilateral and would seek to open markets by threatening retaliation" (Cline 1983: 154). The new strategy is unilateral only if the transgressions of foreign trading partners are ignored. Retaliation by definition occurs to compensate for actions already taken by the other country. What is wrong with seeking to open markets by threatening retaliation if that is the only effective way?

Cline focuses on the possible protectionist outcome of the use of reciprocity. "The principal (legislative) proposals envision U.S. retaliation in the form of higher protection against any foreign country that does not grant comparable market access to U.S. exports" (Cline 1983: 121). He uses a complicated decision-and-outcome scheme to show that the number of times higher barriers would result is greater than the number of times barriers would be reduced. This superficial analysis contains neither a measure of the probabilities of various outcomes nor, even more important, the expected outcome when one of the parties is the United States. Any predicted outcomes from such theoretical exercises that fail to consider the "personalities" involved are useless and misleading. If one of the parties has the market dominance of the United States and a long history of using that power wisely and constructively, the results must surely be better than if some other less responsible country were involved.

It is my view that the use of U.S. market power in this manner in most cases would not lead to higher trade barriers in the United States but rather to the reduction of foreign barriers. Barriers would be reduced not only for U.S. exporters but for all others as well. In those cases where the foreign barrier is not reduced, the imposition of specific, targeted barriers by the United States would be justified. It would remove one of the major threats facing the United States and the rest of the trading world: the imposition with impunity of nontariff and other barriers to trade that nullify the expected benefits of trade liberalization. Thus the results of judicious use of reciprocity legislation by the United States would liberalize the system to benefit all trading nations.

IMPROVING U.S. TRADE LAWS

With the basic reorientation of the U.S. trade posture toward reciprocity, other changes must be made in U.S. laws to accord with the new realities of government-managed trade. U.S. dumping laws need to be revised to address those cases in which the costs of production in the foreign country are essentially determined by arbitrary government decree, fiat, or regulation. Current laws do not adequately provide for situations in which no market exists in the foreign country to determine fair value. These changes would better enable the United States to exclude from the U.S. market those imports that unfairly threaten its own producers.

Similar changes should be made in the countervailing duty (CVD) laws to account for nonmonetary subsidies, for industrial targeting, and for unfairly priced raw materials used in the production processes. Through all of these actions, foreign governments encourage exports at the expense of industries in export markets. The United States is and has been for some time the most vulnerable to these practices, in spite of its CVD laws. These laws need to be tightened and revised in light of the modern practices of foreign governments, which go well beyond traditional monetary subsidies.

Still other changes need to be made in section 301 of the Trade Act of 1974. This section authorizes the president to take action against unfair trade practices. Some improvements were adopted in 1984, but they have not yet been tested. The section is potentially a powerful remedy for government trade management practices. However, its scope needs to be broadened to include trade in services as well as in goods, investment practices in foreign countries that limit opportunities, and unfair trade practices.

The biggest changes necessary relate to the application of these laws. Today, challengers of import dumping, countervailing, or unfair trade practices laws are accused of being protectionist. The implication is that the complainant is as guilty as the respondent. This implication must be removed. Perhaps complaints could be handled without this stigma if the provisions were changed to focus on the specific unfair trading practices.

One effective means to remove this implication may be for the government itself to initiate complaints. This may require the establishment of a new office, akin to the public prosecutors used to enforce criminal law. The new trade prosecutor would be responsible for investigating and then bringing cases whenever U.S. trade laws were violated. Information and data would necessarily be supplied by U.S. industry, but at least a nonprotectionist means of filing suits would be available. In time it would improve the administration of these cases, remove the stigma, and warn foreign nations that unfair trading practices would no longer be tolerated.

A NORTH AMERICAN COMMON MARKET

A natural outgrowth of the business pressures and tendencies now underway would be the consolidation of the economies of North America into a form of common market. This common market would allow the negotiation of special arrangements between the United States, Canada, Mexico, and the countries of Central America and the Caribbean. A great deal of integration has already occurred through the actions of private industry. It is time for governments to recognize these accomplishments and give them explicit political support.

The simplest course to envision is the expansion of the bilateral sectoral discussions with Canada into an exploration of much broader free trade in capital and labor as well as the products in selected sectors. The interdependence of the two economies is now so great that formalizing the relationship to encourage further growth is a small economic step. It is not a small political step for Canada, however, so the initiative must be as much Canadian as U.S. Nevertheless, there are positive signs that Canada may be reaching the political consensus needed to make this commitment. The EEC exists as a common market but its members hold widely differing political views, proving that economic integration can be pursued independently of other goals.

That lesson is even more important for the sensitive issue of political ties with Mexico and Central America. In the short run it is unlikely that these countries will have the freedom of political action to form a common market with the United States. But integration is proceeding now without the support of politicians and it will continue to develop, driven by the imperatives of business.

U.S. manufacturers seek lower cost labor and new markets in the growing countries south of the Rio Grande. Mexico is developing rapidly, not only its oil supplies but also its industry. Much of the new industry is connected to the United States, through U.S. investment in new plants, technology transfer, subcontracting, and component manufacture for U.S.-bound products. Even the Mexican decrees forcing local investment work toward this end. They will result in increased investment by U.S. companies in the Mexican economy, giving larger scope for rationalization and integration of production within North America.

The Caribbean Basin Initiative (CBI) was devised to allow Caribbean and Central American products to enter the United States duty-free for twelve years following its enactment in 1983. The CBI also encourages new U.S. investment in the area. The next step is to make the trade free in both directions, to open the United States to investment and even labor migration from the region. Given the sensitivities in the United States about increased permanent immigration from Mexico and Central America, some form of temporary guest-worker program might be considered, such as the earlier U.S. bracero program (limited to seasonal agricultural workers) or the EEC guest-worker program for industries. But even if this hurdle is insurmountable, as it may be, the establishment of free trade is certainly an attainable goal.

The pressures toward integration are great within the business community. In raw materials, in industrial capacity, in skilled and trainable labor, in high technology and management, the riches of this continent compare favorably with those to be found anywhere, and the businesses know it. They find ways to surmount the barriers, to do business under adverse political conditions, to develop markets supposedly closed to them, and to live with the sometimes absurd local-content rules. Imagine how much greater the growth in all the economies of North America would be if those obstacles were removed. One recent study by a Canadian economist estimates the gains to Canada from bilateral free trade as high as 7 to 10 percent of GNP (Globerman 1984).

It is worth noting that Canada and the United States have had close trading relations for their entire history. There was even a reciprocal trade agreement negotiated in 1855 (but abrogated in 1866) in Canada's own attempt to reduce its reliance on Britain. It led to a growth in trade between two natural trading partners.

In the late 1970s the U.S. Congress mandated a study of the possibility of North American economic integration. The study was conducted by the Commerce Department with assistance from other agencies. It concluded that the time was not yet propitious for a North American common market because of the political problems a U.S. initiative of this type would pose for both Canada and Mexico. With the current discussion of limited free trade between the United States and Canada, some issues are being addressed that can lay the groundwork for a broader arrangement.

Taking a longer view is more encouraging. The United States is becoming more sensitive to the needs and aspirations of its neighbors and will not force the creation of a common market. Canada and Mexico will, in time, see the benefits to their economies as they become more developed. Rationalization of production will continue, resulting from the opportunities a common market provides. It will accelerate the interpenetration of economies that is now occurring without government encouragement.

Looking beyond the continent provides the real reason why a North American common market should exist. The United States, Canada, Mexico, and the Central American and Caribbean countries will face competition from many quarters. Within the broader free trade arrangement, the advanced industrial countries would probably be joined by many of the newly industrial countries. The best way to defend the U.S. position will not be through trade-limiting protectionism, but through greater competition. All of the resources for increasing productivity can be found in North America, but they must be used effectively to achieve results.

The common market will allow that process to occur in the most efficient manner, through the individual decisions of entrepreneurs and business managers. Those decisions will ensure the continued growth of all of the North American economies and their standards of living. In Central America, a common market will be the best defense against totalitarian solutions and outside interference. For the rest it will at last realize the full potential of this vast and rich continent.

15 IMPROVING THE INTERNATIONAL TRADE SYSTEM

Most critics of reciprocity and all defenders of free trade place most of their faith in the GATT. Churchill's comment on democracy could equally apply to the GATT — it is the worst form of government, except for all the others. The GATT has grown along with its responsibilities; it has successfully concluded seven rounds of tariff reductions, and it continues to handle the daily business of conciliating trade disputes between countries. But even its strongest supporters agree that changes need to be made in its coverage, its procedures, and remedies for violation of its provisions.

In 1983 the director general of the GATT, Arthur Dunkel, appointed an international advisory group from seven countries, including the United States, to examine ways to eliminate trade barriers and strengthen the organization. The group recommended eliminating the Multi-Fiber Arrangement, agricultural quotas and preferences, and all other voluntary restraints. It also recommended tightening GATT trade rules on subsidies, trade blocs, and "temporary" protectionist measures. It noted the need for better enforcement of international rules, urging the involvement of trade ministers and regular reviews of members' trade policies, along the lines of the IMF's reviews of members' economic policies. Finally, it recognized the need to wean developing countries away from preferential treatment to begin integrating them more fully into the international system. This group of advisors pointed out some of the major problems facing the GATT.

To better understand the problems of the GATT, consider how it deals with the denial of market opportunities. If a country violates a GATT provision or a tariff agreement, (for instance, a country raises a tariff previously bound at a lower level), then the GATT does not itself impose a penalty. Instead, Article XXIII allows the injured party to withdraw its own concession or take some other action in retaliation. As Dam says, "This remedy underscores the basic principles that the General Agreement is to represent for each contracting party a balance of advantages and that, in the crucial area of tariffs, concessions need be made only in return for equivalent reciprocal concessions" (Dam 1970: 21). GATT's role is merely to authorize the retaliation as being legal.

Of course this role limits the types of disputes that may come before the GATT in this central area of "nullification or impairment" of benefits (the technical terms used in the article). As a result, there have been only two specific cases brought to the GATT under this article since 1947. The first was successfully brought by the Netherlands against U.S. cheese restrictions, in 1952. The other was brought against Japan by the European Economic Community in 1982, claiming wholesale denial of opportunities because of the nontariff barriers inherent in the Japanese economy. As Cline reports, the complaint was so broad in condemning Japan that it was poorly suited for GATT treatment (Cline 1983: 149).

GATT members must approve the request to retaliate under Article XXIII, and as a result it has proved too cumbersome in practice and has fallen into disuse. Cline suggests the revitalization of this article as an alternative to U.S. domestic reciprocity legislation. This would preserve the facade of multilateral action on market access cases.

The problem with that solution lies in the very reason the article has not been used in the past. Agreement that a particular governmental practice or intervention violates the GATT becomes increasingly unlikely as more and more countries adopt the offending practice. Moreover, changing the text of the article to facilitate such complaints would also fail. The GATT operates by consensus, and assuredly the violators like the rules the way they are.

Cline's other suggestions for redressing the imbalances in market access and opportunity involve sector negotiations, negotiations on services and investment, and bilateral negotiations. All of these proposals are no substitute for retaliatory power under reciprocity. Instead, they are forums in which the increased leverage and bargaining power achieved through the reciprocity legislation could be used.

This is not to say there are not other ways in which the GATT can be improved to make it more relevant to today's problems. Many such improvements have been suggested by the United States and are still being pursued.

The United States made a number of constructive proposals for the development of the GATT. It suggested completing the long-standing work on a code to control protectionist actions. But the GATT once again delayed action because of the EEC failure to agree with most other countries. The United States suggested action on a code to control counterfeiting, but negotiations were undertaken at a very slow pace. It also sought discipline over subsidies for agriculture, but again the EEC refused to participate in a work program which might eventually imply the end of its Common Agricultural Policy.

Another U.S. suggestion was that the GATT take steps to prepare for future negotiations in three emerging areas of interest. The United States proposed a study of the services area, which is proceeding, albeit more slowly than had been hoped. The U.S. proposal to begin work on government investment restrictions, which have the effect of limiting or affecting trade, was rejected on the grounds that it lies outside GATT jurisdiction. The real reason was that such investment restrictions are central to the Third World's development planning and political strategy in preparing for the long-postponed North–South negotiations. The final U.S. proposal was for a study of the special problems of high technology industries was the least controversial and therefore was given some lukewarm support.

A number of disputes are brought to the GATT under other articles of the agreement. Improvements can and should be made in the GATT dispute-settlement mechanisms to make them less cumbersome, more certain, and more expeditious. The more fundamental problem, however, is that the GATT is poorly equipped, given the nature of the agreement and the structure of the institution, to deal with the problems raised by government management of trade.

A NEW FREE TRADE ARRANGEMENT

The weaknesses of the GATT in dealing with many forms of managed trade have been described. Its rules fail to provide adequately

for the extensive amount of state trading done by governments and
government-owned enterprises, many of which do not adhere to commercial principles and most of which are protected by monopoly laws.
The GATT also imposes obligations on developing countries, and
countries such as Mexico have refused to join the GATT for fear of
losing their freedom to pursue development policies as they see fit.

A partial solution developed in the Tokyo Round was to negotiate
codes of more limited membership than the full GATT membership.
These codes deal with government procurement, standards, testing,
and other nontariff barriers. Few developing countries accepted the
obligations of the new codes, and thus there exists a three-tier system:
countries completely outside the GATT; countries in the GATT, but
not in the specialized NTB codes; and a few developed countries accepting the NTB codes as well as the general obligations.

What this implies for the future is further balkanization of trading
relationships. Those seeking the most liberal trading environment
have banded together, agreed among themselves the rules they will
apply to each other, and left the rest to join when they can. When a
developing country becomes sufficiently developed to accept the full
disciplines of the codes, it can "graduate" to code membership.

Some may deplore this development as a step toward a breakdown
of the universal multilateral system represented by the GATT. I dis-
agree. It seems, however, a natural outcome of an increasingly com-
plex international economy in which different countries have different, deeply rooted policies. Developed industrial countries, led by the
United States, wish to continue the process of trade liberalization.
Advanced developing countries are not yet ready to accept the liberalization in full, and the poorest countries and the nonmarket countries are in no position to accept them at all. Hence the parting of the
ways.

The code negotiations of the Tokyo Round indicate a much broader
opportunity—to liberalize the international trading system and solve
the problem of government involvement in managing trade. The United States should lead a group of like-minded countries, both developed and developing, into a broad and general free trade area
arrangement that would seek to minimize and eventually eliminate
government intervention. The creation of this new arrangement can
and should be the goal of U.S. trade policy for the remainder of this
century.

The purpose of the group would be to bring together those countries that wish to go beyond the GATT and its codes to establish free

trade among themselves. The group would eliminate tariff barriers, reduce or eliminate nontariff barriers, eliminate quotas, and eliminate all government subsidies, targeting, and other forms of trade management. The group could begin the task by consolidating the gains of the separate codes in one master nontariff barrier agreement and adding to it the specific new obligations of free trade. This arrangement would put Adam Smith's ideal to the test: The general welfare, over time, of the participating countries should increase substantially.

Membership in the free trade arrangement would not derive exclusively from those in the OECD or NATO, but would include developing countries as well. Some European countries probably would want to be members of a U.S.-led free trade bloc. The United States already has made initial overtures to the Caribbean Basin countries, allowing them one-way, duty-free access to the United States; that access should now be made two-way and perpetual. Discussions have also begun for a free trade arrangement between the United States and Israel and an enlarged sectoral free trade arrangement between the United States and Canada; progress is being made.

Since the arrangement need not include geographically contiguous or similar countries, other countries might be expected to join, including from Australasia (the ASEAN group, Korea, and even Japan), Africa, the Middle East, and Latin America (Brazil, Chile, Argentina, Venezuela, and the Caribbean Basin). All of these countries and more are potential members. The main requirement would be to share the belief in the value of free trade to their economies.

Henry Kissinger gave support to this approach in October 1984 when reviewing the international scene. He said:

> If the United States is driven to it, the United States can, however reluctantly, do well at the game of unilateral trade practices and bilateral agreements. In a world of trading blocs, the United States should be able to construct a trading bloc composed of the major Latin American nations, Canada, and probably Australia and New Zealand. Preparation for this partnership should influence American trade and debt policy, especially toward the nations of the Western Hemisphere.
>
> At some point, the sheer weight of the United States managing—in cooperation with like-minded countries—its foreign trade interests with determination and vision will probably convince the rest of the world—to put it politely—of the need for more coordinated trade and economic policies (Kissinger 1984).

The place to start would be with the OECD countries themselves. They have already pledged, in nonbinding ways, to allow free movement of capital and international investment among themselves. Identical pledges on refraining from interference with trade have been discussed in the OECD Trade Committee and it is time to give them reality. The advantage of the OECD is that it provides a forum for the industrialized countries to develop ideas and stimulate change elsewhere. The OECD has proved valuable in developing a consensus on difficult issues yet to be fully addressed in the GATT or other organizations.

But the initiative should not be limited to the OECD. There is excessive bureaucratization in this organization. Its role is to stimulate discussion and studies, not to take action or make decisions. Its strength as a consensus-building organization inhibits negotiating agreements.

Another problem the OECD has yet to solve satisfactorily is the question of membership. What is the OECD to do about the newly industrialized countries, the East bloc, and the OPEC countries, none of which are part of the OECD. For the purposes of the free trade arrangement, these countries must be considered potential participants regardless of their regional or developmental status.

The United States must take the lead in building the free trade arrangement beyond the discussion stage. No other country can be as successful in leading, persuading, cajoling, bargaining, and gaining adherence to the new bloc. Participation in the free trade arrangement would have neither political nor military implications, leaving intact existing blocs of a more formal and political nature. The organizational and legal aspects of the arrangement will have to evolve over time, but they could take the form of a "super-GATT" with concrete, reciprocal, and binding elimination of barriers, backed up by enforceable legal rights exercisable by members.

The reason other countries will participate is simple. The United States will be offering access to its market, the largest and most lucrative in the world. Complete access will be available to those, and only those, who reciprocate. In return they will be required to forgo protections against U.S. and other countries within the free trade arrangement. Those who are not yet prepared to make this bargain will be free to abstain, to remain under the more general obligations and disciplines of the GATT, or even to maintain their current status outside the GATT.

The sole objective of the arrangement would be to realize the benefits of trade liberalization to the maximum extent possible. It would provide the possibility for liberalizing countries to join with like-minded countries in an effective free trade organization. This arrangement would achieve what free traders have long sought, a viable international system truly based on the principles of liberal trade. Without an initiative as sweeping and daring as this, the international trade system is in danger of stagnation as bilateralism and government management of trade rule the day.

BIBLIOGRAPHY

Abernathy, Wayne A. "A Need for Tighter Controls on High Tech Exports." *Backgrounder No. 422.* Washington, D.C.: The Heritage Foundation, 1985.

Baldrige, Malcolm. "The Case for Free Trade." *Export Today* (Spring 1985): 5.

Baldwin, Robert E., ed. *Recent Issues and Initiatives in U.S. Trade Policy,* Cambridge, Mass.: National Bureau of Economic Research, Inc., 1983.

Bale, Harvey E., Jr. "Foreign Investment Policy." Unpublished paper presented at the NOMOS Project Seminar II, The Center for International Affairs, Harvard University, Cambridge, Mass., May 24, 1984.

Bangemann, Martin. Economics Minister of the Federal Republic of Germany, quoted in *International Trade Reporter* 1, no. 7 (August 15, 1984): 178.

Barovick, Richard L. "Opening Government Markets." *Business America* (September 3, 1984): 2.

Bergsten, C. Fred, and Cline, William R. *Trade Policy in the 1980's.* Policy Analyses in International Economics, No. 3. Washington, D.C.: Institute for International Economics, November 1982.

Bradford, Charles H., Project Team Chairman. "Mandate For Leadership: Project Team Report for the Department of Commerce." First Draft, October 31, 1980. Washington, D.C.: The Heritage Foundation, 1980.

Braudel, Fernand. *The Wheels of Commerce.* Translated by Sian Reynolds. New York: Harper & Row, 1982.

Briggs, Jean A. "Back to Barter." *Forbes Magazine* (March 12, 1984): 40.

Brock, Amb. William E. "Trade and Debt: The Vital Linkage." *Foreign Affairs* 62, no. 5 (Summer 1984): 1037.

Brown, Kenneth M. "Protectionism's Latest Guise Examined." *The Journal of Commerce* (July 25, 1984): 4A.

Cantor, David J. "Steel Import Limits: Estimated Import Reductions Under Three Alternative Proposals." Washington, D.C.: Congressional Research Service, The Library of Congress, September 1984.

Cline, William R., ed. *Trade Policy in the 1980s.* Washington: Institute for International Economics, 1983.

———. "Protectionism: An Ill Trade Wind Rises." *The Wall Street Journal,* November 6, 1984, p. 28.

"Clouds Over U.S.–Soviet Trade Are Breaking Up." *Business Week* (December 17, 1984): 44.

Cohen, Robert B. "The Prospects for Trade and Protectionism in the Auto Industry." In *Trade Policy in the 1980s.* Edited by William Cline. Washington, D.C.: Institute for International Economics, 1983.

Czinkota, Michael R. *International Trade and Business in the Late 1980's: An Integrated U.S. Policy Perspective.* Staff Paper #18. Washington, D.C.: National Center for Export–Import Studies, Georgetown University, June 1985.

Czinkota, Michael R., and Marciel, Scot, eds. *U.S.–Arab Economic Relations: A Time of Transition.* New York: Praeger, 1985.

Dam, Kenneth W. *The GATT: Law and International Economic Organization.* Chicago: The University of Chicago Press, 1970.

Davis, Lester A. "New Trade Performance Report Analyzes 1984 U.S. Trade Deficit." *Business America* (July 22, 1985): 10.

Destler, I.M. *Making Foreign Economic Policy.* Washington, D.C.: The Brookings Institution, 1980.

———. "Protectionism and Election-Year Politics: Why Reagan Is a Free-Trade Villain." *New York Times,* March 18, 1984.

Diebold, William, Jr., and Stalson, Helena. "Negotiating Issues in International Services Transactions," In *Trade Policy in the 1980s.* Edited by William Cline. Washington, D.C.: Institute for International Economics, 1983.

Direction of Trade Statistics: Yearbook. Washington, D.C.: International Monetary Fund, 1983.

Dizard, John W. "The Explosion of International Barter." *Fortune,* (February 7, 1983): 88.

Dunkel, Arthur. Address in Hamburg, Germany March 5, 1982. Geneva: GATT Press Release No. 1312, 1982.

"East–West Trade." *Financial Times Report,* December 22, 1983.

Ehrenhaft, Peter D., ed. *Countertrade: International Trade Without Cash.* New York: Law & Business, Inc., 1983.

———. *Countertrade and Trading Companies: Trade Trends in the '80s.* New York: Law & Business, Inc., 1984.

El-Abd, Hesham, and O'Sullivan, Michael Kenney. "Encountering Countertrade." *Journal of Defense & Diplomacy,* (July 1984): 23.

Encyclopaedia Britannica. 11th Edition, 1910–1911.

Federal Register. Ceramic Tile from Mexico, 47, no. 90, May 10, 1982.

"Foreign Investment in the United States: Current Legal and Tax Aspects." Unpublished papers. National Institute Sponsored by the American Bar Association, Chicago, 1982.

Foreign Private Investment in Developing Countries, A Study by the Research Department. Occasional Paper No. 33. Washington, D.C.: International Monetary Fund, 1985.

Fortune Magazine. (September 1949).

Gilder, George. *Wealth and Poverty.* New York: Basic Books Inc., 1981.

———. "Imports Are Not a Problem but a Cure," *The Wall Street Journal,* March 27, 1985, p. 36.

"Global Competition: The New Reality," *The Report of the President's Commission on Industrial Competitiveness,* vol. 1, Washington, D.C., U.S. Government Printing Office, 1985.

Globerman, Steven. "Canada–U.S. Trade Relations: A Current Perspective." Unpublished paper. Faculty of Business Administration, Simon Fraser University, 1984.

Globerman, Steven, and Volpe, John. "Trade Liberalization in the North American Context: Nature, Problems and Prospects." Unpublished paper. National Chamber Foundation, Washington, D.C., 1984.

Goodell, Grace, and Bergner, Jeffrey T. *Conservative Perspectives on Economic Development.* The Heritage Lectures 25. Washington, D.C.: The Heritage Foundation, 1983.

Gotlieb, Amb. Allan E. Remarks on U.S.–Canadian bilateral economic relationship, made to the U.S. Chamber of Commerce Council on Trends and Perspectives, Washington, D.C., February 9, 1984.

Greenhouse, Steven. "The Making of Fortress America." *New York Times,* August 5, 1984, p. F1.

Haendel, Dan. *International Barter and Countertrade.* Washington, D.C.: National Center for Export–Import Studies, Georgetown University, 1984.

Hamilton, Cong. Lee H. "Free Trade: Rhetoric vs. Reality." *Christian Science Monitor,* April 25, 1984, p. 14.

Hanke, Steve H. (pt. 1), and Copper, John F. (pt. 2). "How to Narrow the Trade Gap with Japan." *Backgrounders Nos. 10 and 13.* Washington, D.C.: Asian Studies Center, The Heritage Foundation, 1984.

Hanrahan, Charles E.; Cate, Penelope; and Vogt, Donna U. *Agriculture In the GATT: Toward the Next Round of Multilateral Trade Negotiations.*

Washington, D.C.: Congressional Research Service, The Library of Congress, 1984.

Hansen, Roger D., and Contributors. *U.S. Foreign Policy and the Third World: Agenda 1982.* New York: Praeger Publishers, 1982.

Henretta, James A. *The Evolution of American Society, 1700–1815.* Lexington, Mass.: D. C. Heath and Company, 1973.

Horlick, Gary N.; Bello, Judith Hippler; and Savage, Christopher W. "New Developments in Foreign Government Subsidies." Unpublished manuscript, 1984.

Hormats, Robert D. *Making U.S. International Economic Policy.* Washington, D.C.: National Chamber Foundation, 1984.

———. "Trade Adjustments That All Could Support." *The Wall Street Journal,* September 19, 1984, p. 32.

Hoving, John. "A Piecemeal Smoot–Hawley May Surprise Us All." *New Management* (1984): 22.

Hudgins, Edward L. "An Agenda for the IMF Conference." *Backgrounder No. 381.* Washington, D.C.: The Heritage Foundation, 1984.

———. "Thirteen Myths of a Strong Dollar." *Backgrounder No. 403.* Washington, D.C.: The Heritage Foundation, 1985a.

———. "Why Limiting Textile Imports Would Hurt Americans." *Backgrounder No. 458.* Washington, D.C.: The Heritage Foundation, 1985b.

Hufbauer, Gary Clyde. "Subsidy Issues After the Tokyo Round." In *Trade Policy in the 1980s.* Edited by William Cline. Washington, D.C.: Institute for International Economics, 1983.

Hufbauer, Gary Clyde, and Erb, Joanna Shelton. *Subsidies in International Trade.* Washington, D.C.: Institute for International Economics, 1984.

Hull, Cordell. *Economic Barriers to Peace.* New York: Woodrow Wilson Foundation, 1937.

International Public Policy Foundation. *Technology: World Competition and National Security.* Proceedings of a conference held in Washington, D.C., April 26, 1984.

Johnson, Paul. *Modern Times: The World from the Twenties to the Eighties.* New York: Harper & Row, 1983.

Jones, Kent. "Saving the Steel Industry." *Backgrounder No. 354.* Washington, D.C.: The Heritage Foundation, May 21, 1984.

Kahn, Herman. *The Emerging Japanese Superstate: Challenge and Response.* Englewood Cliffs, N.J.: Prentice-Hall, Inc., 1970.

Kahn, Herman; Brown, William; and Martel, Leon. *The Next 200 Years: A Scenario for America and the World.* New York: William Morrow and Company, Inc. 1976.

Kenwood, A. G., and Lougheed, A. L. *The Growth of the International Economy, 1820–1980.* London: George Allen & Unwin, 1983.

Kissinger, Henry. *White House Years.* Boston: Little Brown and Company, 1979.

———. "International Trade: It's Time to Change the Rules." *The Washington Post,* October 22, 1984, p. A 21.

Klochek, Vasili. "Soviet Foreign Trade in 1982." *Foreign Trade Magazine* no. 5 (1983): 5.

Macdonald, David R. "Reflections of a Heretic: Rethinking U.S. Trade Policy." *Du Pont Context* 13, no. 1 (1984): 10.

Manzhulo, A. N. "Mutually Advantageous Trade and Economic Cooperation Between the USSR and Other Countries: Results and Prospects." *Foreign Trade Magazine* no. 7 (1983): 35.

Maurois, Andre. *Disraeli: A Picture of the Victorian Age.* Translated by Hamish Miles. New York: Time Incorporated, 1928.

McKenzie, Richard B. "National Industrial Policy: An Overview of the Debate." *Backgrounder No. 275.* Washington, D.C.: The Heritage Foundation, 1983.

McKinsey & Company, Inc. *Japan Business Obstacles and Opportunities.* Tokyo: President Inc., 1983.

Ministry of International Trade and Industry, Government of Japan. *"Trade and Industrial Policy for the 1970s."* Tokyo, 1971.

———. "Japan's Industrial Policy: A Long-Range Vision." Tokyo, 1974.

———. "MITI's Vision of International Trade and Industry Policies for the 1980's." Tokyo, 1980.

Munger, Michael C., and Rehbein, Kathleen A. "The High Cost of Protectionism." *Europe* (May/June 1984): 10.

Naisbitt, John. *Megatrends: Ten New Directions Transforming Our Lives.* New York: Warner Books, Inc., 1982.

"New Restrictions on World Trade." *Business Week* (July 19, 1982): 118.

Nixon, Richard. *The Real War.* New York: Warner Books, 1981.

"Noah's Ark, Anyone?" *Forbes* (August 12, 1985).

Novak, Jeremiah. "The New Geopolitics: The North American Common Market—A Conceptual Background Study Report." Unpublished manuscript, 1979.

Olmer, Lionel H. *U.S. Manufacturing at a Crossroads.* Washington, D.C.: U.S. Department of Commerce, 1985.

———. "High Technology and GATT: The Key International Trade Issue Facing the United States and Europe." *Business America,* August 20, 1984, p. 2.

"OPEC Current and Capital Accounts." New York: Bankers Trust Company, January 1983.

Patterson, Gardner. *Discrimination in International Trade: The Policy Issues 1945-65.* Princeton: Princeton University Press, 1966.

Protectionism: Threat to International Order, The Impact on Developing Countries. Report by a Group of Experts. London: Commonwealth Secretariat, 1982.

Rashish, Myer. "The International Impact of American Economic Policy."

Remarks to the Financial Times Conference on "World Banking in 1983", London, December 9, 1982.

Reagan, Pres. Ronald W. Remarks to the joint annual meeting of the International Monetary Fund and the World Bank, *New York Times,* September 26, 1984, p. D 5.

Rector, Robert. "A New Strategy for East-West Trade." *Backgrounder No. 357.* Washington, D.C.: The Heritage Foundation, 1984.

Reich, Robert B. *The Next American Frontier.* New York: Penguin Books, 1984.

———. "Beyond Free Trade." *Foreign Affairs* 61, no. 4 (Spring 1983): 774.

Roth, Sen. William V., Jr. "A Battle Plan for the Trade War." Remarks at the National Press Club, Washington, D.C., February 22, 1983.

Rutter, John. "Recent and Future Trends in International Direct Investment." *Business America* (August 6, 1984): 3.

Saferian, A.E. "Trade Related Investment Issues." In *Trade Policy in the 1980s.* Edited by William Cline. Washington, D.C.: Institute for International Economics, 1983.

Samuelson, Robert J. "Delusions Over Trade," *The Washington Post,* December 19, 1984, p. B 1.

Schlossstein, Steven. *Trade War: Greed, Power, and Industrial Policy on Opposite Sides of the Pacific.* New York: Congdon & Weed, Inc., 1984.

Scott, Bruce R., and Lodge, George C. *U.S. Competitiveness in the World Economy: A Problem of Premises.* Working Paper, Division of Research, Harvard Business School, Boston, Mass., September 1984.

"Sell American: Proposals for the Revival of United States Foreign Trade and Investment." 1984 Policy Declaration, National Foreign Trade Council, New York, 1984.

Shelp, Ronald Kent. *Beyond Industrialization: Ascendancy of the Global Service Economy.* New York: Praeger Publishers, 1981.

Simon, William E. *A Time for Truth.* New York: Reader's Digest Press, 1978.

Soros, George. "The International Debt Problem: Diagnosis and Prognosis." New York: Morgan Stanley Investment Research, July 1983.

Stanley, Timothy W.; Danielian, Ronald L.; and Rosenblatt, Samuel M. *U.S. Foreign Economic Strategy for the Eighties.* Boulder, Colorado: Westview Press, 1982.

Starrels, John. "Strengthening a Vital Partnership." *Europe* (March/April, 1984): 12.

Sterngold, James. "A Nation Hooked on Foreign Funds." *New York Times,* November 18, 1984, p. P 1.

Sullivan, Scott. "The Decline of Europe." *Newsweek* (April 9, 1984): 44.

Trade and Payments Division. *The Rise in Protectionism.* Washington, D.C.: International Monetary Fund, 1978.

"Trends in United States Foreign Trade." *Economic Road Maps,* nos. 1942–1943. New York: The Conference Board, January 1983.

United Nations Conference on Trade and Development. "Protectionism and Structural Adjustment: Anti-dumping and Countervailing Duty Practices." TD/B/, Geneva, January 4, 1984.

U.S. Congress. Senate. Associate Director, U.S. General Accounting Office, Allan I. Mendelowitz, Testimony on International Rules Governing Trade. Subcommittee on International Economic Policy, Senate Committee on Foreign Relations, June 15, 1984.

U.S. Department of Commerce. *Current International Trade Position of the United States.* Washington, D.C., February 1984.

———. "Trading with the U.S.S.R." Overseas Business Reports 77-38, April 19, 1983a.

———. International Trade Administration. *Doing Business with China.* Washington, D.C., 1983b.

———. International Trade Administration. *U.S. Competitiveness in the International Economy.* Washington, D.C., 1981.

U.S. International Trade Commission. *36th Quarterly Report to the Congress and the Trade Policy Committee on Trade Between the United States and the Nonmarket Economy Countries During July–September 1983.* USITC Publication 1468, Washington, D.C., 1983.

U.S. Department of State. International Sugar Agreement, 1977; International Coffee Agreement, 1976; International Tin Agreement, 1977; International Natural Rubber Agreement, 1979; International Agreement on Jute and Jute Products, 1982; International Cocoa Agreement, 1980. U.S. Treaty Series.

U.S. News & World Report. Interview with Amb. William E. Brock, U.S. Trade Representative, April 8, 1985, p. 72.

Verzariu, Pompiliu. *International Countertrade: A Guide for Managers and Executives.* Washington, D.C.: U.S. Department of Commerce, 1984.

Volpe, John. Letter to members of the Council on Trends and Perspectives of the National Chamber Foundation, June 6, 1986.

Waldmann, Raymond J. *Foreign Policy Export Controls: Proposals for Change.* Charlottesville, Va.: Center for Law and National Security, University of Virginia, 1984.

———. *International Codes of Conduct: Regulating International Business.* Washington, D.C.: The American Enterprise Institute, 1979a.

———. *Investment Incentive Programs of the Pacific Basin.* Los Angeles: University of Southern California, Graduate School of Business, 1979b.

Waldmann, Raymond J., and Cohn, Robert A. *Business Investment in the United States.* Rev. ed. Washington, D.C.: The Bureau of National Affairs, 1984.

Waldmann, Raymond J., and Mansbach, B. Thomas. *Investment Incentive Programs in Western Europe.* Washington, D.C.: U.S. Chamber of Commerce, 1978.

Wallis, Allen. "Commodity Markets and Commodity Agreements." Address before the National Coffee Association, February 11, 1986. Current Policy No. 791, U.S. Department of State, Washington, D.C.

Walsh, James I. "Countertrade: Not Just for East-West An/ More." *Journal of World Trade Law* (January/February 1983): 3.

Walter, Ingo. "Structural Adjustment and Trade Policy in the International Steel Industry." In *Trade Policy in the 1980s.* Edited by William Cline. Washington, D.C.: Institute for International Economics, 1983.

Wanniski, Jude. *The Way the World Works: How Economies Fail—and Succeed.* New York: Basic Books, Inc., 1978.

Wasinger, Tom. "Fashioning an Industrial Relief Act." *The Wall Street Journal,* June 21, 1984.

Wiedenbaum, Murray L. "Free Trade Under Attack: What America Can Do." von Mises Memorial Lecture, Hillsdale College (reprinted in *imprimis,* Hillsdale College, Hillsdale Mich., vol. 13, no. 7, July 1984.

Wiedenbaum, Murray L.; with Munger, Michael C.; and Penoyer, Ronald J. *Toward a More Open Trade Policy.* St. Louis: Center for the Study of American Business, Washington University, 1984.

Weigand, Robert E. "Apricots for Ammonia: Barter, Clearing, Switching, and Compensation in International Business." *California Management Review* (Fall 1979): 33.

The White House, Office of the Press Secretary. Memorandum for the United States Trade Representative—Subject: Steel Import Relief Determination. September 18, 1984.

Wilcox, Clair. *A Charter for World Trade.* New York: Macmillan, 1949.

Wolf, Martin. "Managed Trade in Practice: Implications of the Textile Arrangements." In *Trade Policy in the 1980s.* Edited by William Cline. Washington, D.C.: Institute for International Economics, 1983.

"The World's In-House Traders." *The Economist* (March 1, 1986).

"The Worldwide Steel Industry: Reshaping to Survive." *Business Week* (August 20, 1984): 150.

"The Yankee Trader: Death of a Salesman?" *U.S. News & World Report* (April 8, 1985).

Zhuravlev, Gennadi. "65th Anniversary of the Foreign Trade State Monopoly." *Foreign Trade Magazine* no. 4 (1983): 2.

Zinoviev, N.V. "Soviet-American Trade and Economic Relations: Problems and Perspectives." *Journal of the U.S.-USSR Trade and Economic Council* (1983): 6.

INDEX

Iran, 120, 133, 154
Iran–Iraq War, 97
Ireland, 71
Israel, 75, 81
Italy, 6, 20, 31, 70, 73, 89; auto quota,
  117; investment incentives, 128;
  services, 120

Jackson-Vanik Amendment, 146
Jamaica, 155
Japan, xi, 4, 6, 7, 8, 26, 31, 38, 53–67,
  69, 74, 79, 91, 104, 112, 163, 167,
  178, 181; automobile trade, 47, 114,
  115, 116; baseball bats, 62; countertrade, 153, 155; export credits, 89;
  export laws, 55; GATT membership, 104; gross national product,
  13; important industries, 56;
  industry rationalization, 55; interest
  rates, 92; machine tool industry, 62;
  Meiji Restoration, 54; Ministry of
  Commerce and Agriculture, 54;
  Ministry of Commerce and
  Industry, 54; Ministry of Finance,
  57; Ministry of International Trade
  and Industry (MITI), 46, 54–57 (see
  also); Ministry of Munitions, 56;
  nontariff barriers, 60; overbuilt
  industries, 58; postwar growth, 53;
  services, 120; soda ash imports, 61;
  state ownership, 27; steel, 109;
  structurally depressed industries, 57;
  targeting, 65; tariffs, 39; war aims,
  27–9; World War II, 54–6
Japan Development Bank, 57
Japan Export-Import Bank, 57
Japan Society for the Promotion of
  Machine Industry, 65
Jefferson, Thomas, 22
Joint Commissions (for trade
  promotion), 141; US–China, 141;
  US–USSR, 141

Kennedy, John F., 104
Kennedy Round, position of Poland, 144
Kissinger, Henry A., 166, 181
Komatsu, 153
Korea, 27, 110, 112, 125, 181; gross
  national product, 13; services, 120;
  steel industry, 109
Kuwait, 98, 125
Kuwait Oil Company, 12

Latin America, 26, 164, 181;
  compensation agreements, 151;
  performance requirements, 128
Latin American Free Trade Area (1961),
  71, 78
Latin American–European Trade, 78
League of Nations, 28
Lenin, V. I., 136; system of foreign
  trade, 140
Leontief, Wassily, 121
Less Developed Countries (LDC):
  GATT treatment, 166
Lewis, Drew, 115
Liberal Democratic Party (Japan), 61
Local Content Bill (autos), 117
Lome Convention, 74
London–Bombay Shipping Conference,
  123
Long-Term Arrangement (textiles), 103
Luxembourg, 70; customs union with
  Belgium, 73

Machine Tool Exports, 64–66
Malaysia, 26, 79; bilateral investment
  treaty, 130
Malmgren, Harald, 113
Managed Trade, xi–xiii, 41–2, 95–6;
  alternatives to, 167; barter and
  countertrade, 149–59; military
  procurement, 156–9; origins of,
  42–44; sectoral agreements, 103;
  Soviet system, 131, 136–9; steel,
  108–14; textile trade, 104; under
  GATT, 41; United States views, 166
Manchuria, 27, 56
Market Disruption, 104
Marshall Fields, 12
Marshall Plan, 33, 164
Material Injury, 85
McDonnell Douglas, 93, 151–2, 157
McDonalds, 119
Meat Board of New Zealand, 154
Meiji Restoration, 27
Mercantilist System, 19–21
Metal Fasteners, 9
Mexico, 7, 80, 88, 113, 128, 155, 169,
  173–4; investment protection, 174;
  relation to U.S., 175; services, 120;
  steel, 109
Michelin Company, 87
Middle Ages, 19–20
Middle East, 181

ABOUT THE AUTHOR

Raymond J. Waldmann is Director of Government Affairs for the Boeing Commercial Airplane Co., Seattle. He is responsible for trade policies, legislative affairs, and relations with the U.S. and foreign governments.

Waldmann has served in the U.S. government in many capacities. Most recently, as Assistant Secretary of Commerce for International Economic Policy in the Reagan administration, he was responsible for trade and investment policy, East–West trade, the policies and programs of the Foreign Commercial Service in sixty-seven countries, negotiations with major U.S. trading partners, and representation at the GATT and the OECD. He helped develop the Commerce Department's position on trade legislation, including the Export Trading Company Act and the Foreign Corrupt Practices Act. Waldmann was also a member of the boards of the Overseas Private Investment Corporation (OPIC) and the Ex-Im Bank. As Deputy Assistant Secretary of State for Economic and Business Affairs, Waldmann negotiated intergovernmental agreements on aviation, shipping, communications, and technology. On the White House Staff under presidents Nixon and Ford, Waldmann developed policies for federal budgets, urban growth, science and technology, international economics, and foreign intelligence.

In the private sector Waldmann practiced law in Washington, was counsel to the Chicago firm of Schiff, Hardin & Waite, and consulted with the management consulting firm of Harbridge House, Boston. As a management consultant with Arthur D. Little, Inc. in its Boston, London, and Brussels offices, he specialized in economic development and marketing projects, consulting with corporations, governments, and development agencies in the United States and abroad.

Waldmann is the author of numerous publications on international investment and finance, including *Direct Investment and Development in the U.S., Foreign Trade Zones in the U.S., Investment Incentive Programs in Western Europe, International Codes of Conduct,* and *Investment Incentive Programs of the Pacific Basin.* He holds degrees in chemical engineering and humanities from the Massachusetts Institute of Technology and in law from Harvard University.